THE
RATIONALE
OF CENTRAL
BANKING

T0125169

Vera C. Smith

THE
RATIONALE
OF CENTRAL
BANKING
and the
Free Banking
Alternative

PREFACE BY LELAND B. YEAGER

Liberty Fund

This book is published by Liberty Fund, Inc., a foundation established to encourage study of the ideal of a society of free and responsible individuals.

The cuneiform inscription that serves as our logo and as the design motif for our endpapers is the earliest-known written appearance of the word "freedom" (*amagi*), or "liberty." It is taken from a clay document written about 2300 B.C. in the Sumerian city-state of Lagash.

Library of Congress Cataloging-in-Publication Data

Smith, Vera C., 1912–1976
    [Rationale of central banking]
    The rationale of central banking and the free banking alternative
Vera C. Smith; preface by Leland B. Yeager.
    p.   cm.
    Reprint. Originally published: The rationale of central banking.
Westminster, England: P.S. King & Son Ltd., 1936.
    Includes bibliographical references.
    1. Banks and banking, Central.   2. Banks and banking, Central—
Europe—History.   3. Banks and banking, Central—United States—
History.
HG1811 .S5   1990
332.1'1'094—dc20   90-30937
                                                            CIP

ISBN 0-86597-086-6
ISBN 0-86597-087-4 (pbk.)

93 19 20 21 22 C 6 5 4 3 2
19 20 21 22 23 P 7 6 5 4 3

Contents

be concentrated in the Bank of England; as early as 1825 the Bank was looked upon as the "lender of last resort" • The agitation for joint stock banking; third period of greater freedom for note issuing in the provinces; deposit banking opened to free competition in London as well as in the country • Increasing tendency to centralisation of gold reserves and then to centralisation of banking reserves • Antagonism towards joint stock note-issuing banks; the Bank's reluctance to acknowledge its influence on the operations of other banks • Fourth period after 1844; consolidation of the centralised systems.

and monopoly • Second experiment with a central bank (the First Bank of the U.S.) • The 1814 suspensions • Political influences • The lack of branches and of clearing facilities • The third attempt to maintain a central institution (the Second Bank of the U.S.); the suspensions of 1836 and 1839 • The extreme laxity with which insolvency was treated • Attempts to deal with over-expansions and suspensions (a) the more frequent return of notes secured by the Suffolk bank system and the Massachusetts law; (b) penalties for suspension; (c) special security for note holders; prior liens on assets; double liability; the New York safety fund system • The "free banking" law of New York • The Civil War and the general application of the bond deposit system by the National Bank Act.

The late development of modern banking business • The first semi-State bank in Prussia • Competition of private banks • 1833 onwards—Treasury monopoly of the note issue • The policy in Bavaria and Saxony • The growth of the *Bankfreiheitspartei* in the 'forties; the scarcity of capital and the idea that banks possess "magic power"; the *crédit mobilier* idea; the genuine scarcity of note currency • This and the issues of notes by the border States led to a reorganisation of the Royal Bank • The continual agitation secured at last some concessions for private note-issuing banks • Joint stock banks in *crédit mobilier* business • Slow development of note-issuing banks; the notes of the border States again the motive for slight modifications in the restrictions on private note-issuing banks • The reaction in favour of central banking beginning with the crisis of 1857; the 1866 crisis and emphasis on central bank aid; deposit banking given freedom by the reform of the law on joint stock companies; the realisation of the importance of discount policy • All these factors led up to the foundation of the Reichsbank.

ated • Competition in banking demanded by Coq, Chevalier, Mannequin • Limited plurality on a departmental basis proposed by Lavergne • The most prominent disputants • Wolowski *versus* Chevalier • The evidence before the *Banque Enquête* • The anti-inflation school • Emile de Laveleye attacked the inflationist group of free bankers • Cernuschi and Modeste attacked bank notes in general • Summary of the central banking case by Coullet • Summary of the free banking case by Horn • Later publications of Wolowski, Chevalier, Courcelle-Seneuil • Juglar's argument for a central clearing bank within a competitive system • The connection between the free banking and banking schools.

ties • The English reactions to the adoption of a discount policy by the Bank of France; *The Economist* and Goschen; support of the Pereire doctrines by Patterson; Guthrie's attack on the Bank of England monopoly; attack on fiduciary issues by Phillips • The general question of unity *versus* plurality • Bagehot's evidence and J. S. Mill's memorandum to the French Commission • Bagehot's analysis of effects of the single reserve system and the "lender of the last resort" theory of central banking • Table of cross groupings between central *versus* free banking and banking *versus* currency school adherents.

The American system at the beginning of the twentieth century • Differences between the American system and free banking proper • (a) prohibition of branches; (b) bond deposit system of note issue which encouraged banks to get loans out by deposit credit for preference, with consequent difficulties if the public wanted notes instead of deposits • Long-run trend in the note issue • Short-run inflexibility • Sluggishness of redemption • Crises with suspensions of cash payments • The deficiencies of the American system were attributed to the inelasticity of note issue, to inelastic reserve policy, and to lack of economy in the use of reserves • Attempts to remedy the latter by the clearing house loan certificate, and by Treasury relief • The need for a Government fiscal agent • The high cost of check collection • The 1907 crisis and the Aldrich-Vreeland Act to provide emergency currency • The work of the Monetary Commission • Swing of opinion in favour of a permanent central banking institution.

The acceptance of central banking • The main differences between central and free banking systems • Mo-

nopoly of note issue and centralisation of reserves • Free
banking defined • Strict enforcement of obligations pre-
cludes a general abandonment of the gold standard, but a
central bank can resort to legalised bankruptcy • Free
banking keeps the banks' policy closely dependent on
movements in gold reserves • The case for and against—
connections with the banking *versus* currency controversy • The free banking thesis is not necessarily bound
up with banking school doctrines • Protection of the
small note holder argument • The comparative tendencies to expansion • Arguments of the central bankers that
an external drain affects all banks whether they expand
or not • Argument of the free bankers that there is an automatic mechanism of control via clearings; how far this
can be sustained; argument of central bankers that there
are no conservative banks because the profit motive
causes all banks to join in an expansion • Argument for a
lender of last resort • Application of these arguments to
the cases of (a) small notes and (b) deposit banking • Modern arguments for central banking and tendencies in the
theory of central banking: (a) pursuit of a rational monetary policy; (b) international co-operation • Final remarks
on comparative tendencies of the two systems in causing
disturbances • Future policy • Tendencies towards extension of control to deposit banking.

Preface

Vera Smith's *The Rationale of Central Banking* invites us to reassess our monetary institutions and give reform proposals due consideration. The decades since it first appeared in 1936 have restored its themes to relevance. Government-dominated monetary systems have continued to perform poorly. Other experience, as well as the work of James Buchanan and the Public Choice School, has heightened skepticism about government generally. People are now willing to discuss what Vera Smith set out to examine: "the relative merits of a centralized monopolistic banking system and a system of competitive banks all possessing equal rights to trade" (p. 3).

After a biographical sketch of Vera Smith, I survey the leading themes of her book. I then offer some embroidery on them and consider how they bear on current issues of money and banking reform.

Vera Smith wrote *The Rationale of Central Banking* as a doctoral dissertation at the University of London School of Economics under the supervision of Friedrich A. Hayek. She received her Ph.D. degree there in 1935, having enrolled as an undergraduate in 1930. She studied with Hayek, Lionel Robbins, T. E. Gregory, J. R. Hicks, and Dennis Robertson; in 1933–34 she was Hugh Dalton's research assistant. Thanks not only to the school's faculty but also to a group of students who, like herself, were to become renowned economists, Smith experienced the London School in what were perhaps its golden years. In 1936–37 Smith served as economic assistant at the Imperial Economic Committee.

In April 1937, Smith married the German economist Friedrich Lutz, who was an assistant to Walter Eucken in Freiburg and had held a fellowship of the Rockefeller Foundation in England in 1934–35. In the year of their marriage Friedrich Lutz received another Rockefeller fellowship, and the couple traveled to the United States. After a year and a half back in Europe, the Lutzes returned to the United States just before the outbreak of World War II. (Lutz's traditional-liberal orientation blocked him from an academic career in Nazi Germany.) During the war Vera Lutz served on the research staffs first of the International Finance Section of Princeton University and then of the League of Nations, also in Princeton. In the latter post Vera Lutz worked with such noted economists as Alexander Loveday, Gottfried Haberler, and Ragnar Nurkse.

From 1939 to 1953 Friedrich Lutz held positions from instructor to full professor at Princeton University. After a year in 1951–52 as visiting professor at Freiburg, in 1953 he moved to the University of Zurich, where he taught until retiring in 1972. He was a visiting professor at Yale in the winter of 1962–63. From 1950 to 1963 Mrs. Lutz spent frequent periods for research at the Bank of Italy, the development agency for southern Italy, and the Banca Nationale del Lavoro. From 1963 to 1969 she frequently visited Paris for research on French indicative planning. She never chose to accept a teaching position. Professor Lutz died in Zurich in 1975; Mrs. Lutz, born at Faversham, Kent, England, on 28 April 1912, died in Zurich on 20 August 1976.[1]

[1] Biographical and bibliographical facts come mainly from articles assembled by Ente per gli Studi Monetari, Bancari e Finanziari "Luigi Einaudi," 1984, especially those by Rosaria Giuliani Gusman and Gottfried Haberler; from Verena Veit-Bachmann's article on Friedrich Lutz; and from a letter and enclosure dated 26 June 1989 written by Mrs. Brenda K. Fowler, the sister of Vera Smith

Vera and Friedrich Lutz were both prominent members of the Mont Pelerin Society, and Friedrich was its president from 1964 to 1967. The Society's international membership consists mainly of scholars but includes journalists and business people also. It was established under the leadership of F. A. Hayek in 1947 with the purpose of fighting socialism and revitalizing classical liberalism.

The Lutzes collaborated on several works, including *Monetary and Foreign Exchange Policy in Italy* (1950) and *The Theory of Investment of the Firm* (1951). Books written by Mrs. Lutz alone include *Italy, a Study in Economic Development* (1962) and *Central Planning for the Market Economy: An Analysis of the French Theory and Experience* (1969). Besides writing many articles on money, credit, banking, public finance, the theory of the firm, economic development, economic planning, and the labor market, Mrs. Lutz translated books by Wilhelm Röpke, Oskar Morgenstern, and Fritz Machlup from German into English.

A central bank, as Smith notes, is not a product of natural development. It originates through government favors and bears special privileges and responsibilities. Typically, it serves as banker for the government and for the ordinary banks and monopolizes or dominates the issue of paper money. From this privilege derive the secondary functions and characteristics of a modern central bank: it guards the bulk of its country's gold reserve, and its notes and deposits form a large portion of the cash reserves of ordinary banks. It is constrained under a gold standard, though less tightly than competing banks would be, by the obligation to keep its notes redeemable. When unable to meet this obligation, it typically suspends payments and goes off the gold standard, while its notes acquire forced currency. (One excuse for such actions is that reserves held with it can be guaranteed

Lutz. I am grateful to Mrs. Fowler for going to the trouble of preparing her valuable information.

safe only if its notes remain in circulation even with their redemption suspended.) Control over the volume of its own note and deposit issue gives the central bank power over the size or scale of the country's money and banking system and over the general credit situation.

Smith touches on the aims and origins of central banks. A central bank may originate as a privately owned profit-seeking institution. Another motivation, not incompatible with the first, is to help in the financing of government. Smith reminds us of that reason for establishment of the Bank of England, and she shows similar motivations at work in France and elsewhere.

The special privileges and dominant position of a central bank thrust responsibilities onto it that dilute or override its profit orientation. This is true of fully evolved central banks like today's Bank of England and the Federal Reserve System in the United States. As "lender of last resort," the central bank is supposed to come to the rescue of the ordinary banks during shortages of reserve funds and scramblings for currency, lending them its own freshly issued bank notes. Disregarding narrow profit considerations, it is supposed to use its influence over money, credit, and interest rates to serve public objectives such as, before 1914, keeping the country's currency firmly on the gold standard and, nowadays, resisting inflation while promoting production and employment (to the extent that those objectives are feasible and compatible).

Free banking, as Smith defines it, is a regime allowing banks to operate and even to issue bank notes under no restrictions beyond compliance with general company law (pp. 169–170). A bank may enter the field without special permission if it can show profit prospects, raise sufficient capital, and win public confidence in itself and its notes. It has the same rights and responsibilities as other business enterprises. Its notes are "promises to pay," redeemable in

whatever the basic money might be (under the gold standard, this is gold or instruments redeemable at full value in
gold). As Smith points out, "A general abandonment of the
gold standard is inconceivable under these conditions"
(p. 170). No bank could keep irredeemable notes in circulation by having them declared legal tender. Any bank suspending redemption would be declared bankrupt and
liquidated, its assets being applied to meet the claims of its
creditors. Stockholders would lose all or part of their
investment.

Smith reviews the banking histories of England, Scotland,
France, Germany, and the United States. She also surveys
controversies in these countries, mainly in the nineteenth
century, over whether a central bank with its distinctive responsibilities and powers is desirable or, on the contrary,
private banks might advantageously be left free of central
domination. (She sets aside, as she notes, a review of Italian
and Spanish writings.) She reviews by countries rather than
by topics, presumably finding it convenient to group together the arguments of writers who were largely commenting on each other's writings.

Smith cross-groups writers into four camps (as in her table
on page 144–145) according to their acceptance of the doctrines of either the currency school or the banking school
and their advocacy of either central banking or free banking. The first two schools are mainly associated with British
monetary debates from the 1820s on.[2] The currency school
accepted the quantity theory of money and generally
wanted to make a mixed system of gold and paper currency
behave much as pure gold money would have done. The
banking school accepted doctrines tinged with fallacy, doctrines about "real bills," about accommodating the quantity

[2] See Anna J. Schwartz (1987), under the reference listing that follows, for a
discussion of different schools. Subsequent in-text citations are to references in
this listing.

of money, even over the business cycle, to changes in the supposed needs of trade, and about a supposed automatic reflux of excessive bank notes.

The controversy over free versus central banking is distinct, says Smith (pp. 171–172, 176): it raises arguments additional to and independent of the points disputed by the banking and currency schools. Both Lawrence White (1984) and Anna Schwartz (1987) have since collapsed Smith's four categories into three: the free-banking school, the currency school, and the banking school. Perhaps the explanation is that White and Schwartz dealt almost exclusively with British controversies, whereas Smith extended her study to the continent. Few writers seem to have adhered to the currency and free-banking schools both, but Smith did find at least the Germans Otto Michaelis and Otto Huebner, the Austrian Ludwig von Mises, and the Frenchman Henri Cernuschi in that position. As she says (p. 176), theirs could be a perfectly consistent position so far as they aimed at checking fluctuations in the volume of money and credit.

Historically, support for central banking was more closely connected with the currency than with the banking school, and the currency school's success in theoretical controversy was claimed as a victory for central banking as well. The free-banking school came under suspicion, especially in France, for placing so much emphasis on banking-school ideas, even inflationary ideas, including the denial of the quantity theory and claims that bank notes cannot be issued in excess provided that they are issued by way of loans of appropriate kinds (p. 172).

The banking school placed ill-conceived emphasis on bankable assets. Smith repeatedly uses the German term *bankmässige Deckung*, evidently regarding it as untranslatable. Literally, it means "bankwise cover" and refers to the idea that a bank's monetary liabilities should be matched by holdings of suitable assets. These, according to the notorious "real-bills doctrine," were quintessentially short-term, self-liquidating commercial and industrial loans, loans to finance the production or marketing of additional goods within a very few months. Banking conducted on such a principle would properly match the money supply to the supply of goods coming to market. Besides overlooking the fallacy of composition involved, the banking school ignored the point that not even a merely short-term general overissue of bank notes can be quickly remedied without disturbing business conditions. It was just such disturbances that the currency school aimed at preventing (pp. 173–174).

The supposed principles of bankable assets and especially of automatic reflux of excessive notes might have a certain validity applied to a free-banking system, but they would not apply to a centralized system. The difference involves competing banks' demands for settlement of claims on each other and the restraint posed by adverse clearing balances (p. 174 and later in chapter XII). In practice, a centralized fiduciary note issue constrained by a fixed limit and a decentralized system with gold convertibility would not differ greatly in their results.

Smith interprets Walter Bagehot as adopting a compromise view (p. 143). He found Britain's banking system anomalous—not what people would have deliberately designed from scratch. But it existed, and Britons had to make the best of it by clearly recognizing its weaknesses and having the Bank of England accept its attendant responsibilities and hold reserves adequate for meeting them.

In her concluding chapter especially, Smith reconsiders the main arguments on central banking versus free banking. This reconsideration was necessary, for "the superiority of central banking over the alternative system became a dogma which never again came up for discussion and was accepted without question or comment in all the later foundations of central banks" (p. 167). For answers to most of these arguments, the reader should see Smith's own discussion.

One argument against free banking is that the notes of a particular bank do not remain in the hands of the persons who dealt with it voluntarily, as by borrowing from it. Routine circulation thrusts them even onto persons scarcely in a position to discriminate between good and bad notes. The government should therefore impose some uniformity onto the note issue (p. 177).

A second argument concerns monetary expansions and contractions, leading to inflations and depressions. "Any attempt to make a final evaluation of the relative merits of alternative systems of banking must look primarily to the tendencies they manifest towards instability, or more particularly to the amount of causal influence they exert in cyclical fluctuations" (p. 192). Opponents of free banking (such as Mountifort Longfield, discussed below) argued that aggressively expanding banks might impose the burden of restraint, or even the necessity of going out of business, onto more conservative banks (pp. 85–88, 177–178).

A third argument holds a central bank better able than competing banks to command public confidence and to cope with crises, as by serving as lender of last resort (pp. 185ff). A fourth argument finds a central authority necessary for a "rational" monetary policy (pp. 189–190); a fifth regards central banks as essential to international monetary cooperation (p. 190).

These last two arguments had become in Smith's time "the almost exclusively motivating reasons for the foundations of new central banks" (p. 192). Modern thinking tended to favor "intelligent planning" over automatic rules. A related argument presumably at work, as in the establishment of the Federal Reserve System in the United States, is one Smith does not state explicitly: other countries already have central banks. Why remain backward or out of step?

Nowadays, furthermore, it seems reasonable to suppose that central banks are valued for providing prestigious and comfortable jobs.

Before turning to specific issues of monetary reform, let us ponder what Smith calls "by far the most important controversial point in the theory of free banking" (p. 88; cf. pp. 85–88, 177–185, 197–199). She attributes the controversy to Mountifort Longfield, who, in an article of February 1840, imagined a system of two banks initially doing the same volume of business and holding equal gold reserves. Now one bank aggressively expands its loans and note issue. Later on, as the public starts demanding gold, let us say for export after the monetary expansion and resulting price inflation has caused a balance-of-payments deficit, the public will not selectively present the notes of the guilty bank for redemption. This demand falls, rather, on both banks. As a result, the gold reserve of the bank that did not increase its note circulation falls in greater proportion than its circulation. If this moderate bank wishes to restore its original reserve ratio, it must shrink its volume of business, which, however, enables its aggressive rival to expand even further. The moderate bank may be driven out of business altogether, unless it too expands aggressively in self-defense.

To generalize: a country with several or many note-issuing banks will suffer under alternations of business excitement and depression, of high and low prices. A bank will gain most by expanding during the period of excitement and being quick to contract as the panic arrives. A system more injurious to a country's prosperity could scarcely be devised.

Smith examines this argument in her concluding chapter; some restatement and interpretation may be in order here. One flaw in Longfield's argument, she says, is that it overlooks how continuous expansion by one group of banks and contraction by the moderate group will cause an increasing

xxii   THE RATIONALE OF CENTRAL BANKING

proportion of the gold outflow to impinge on the expanding banks' reserves, which will be exhausted before the moderate banks have been driven out of business.

A relatively minor flaw in Longfield's argument was his stress on the return flow to an expanding bank of its own and other banks' notes as its borrowing customers repay their loans. That strand of the argument neglected the lag between the granting and the repayment of loans, an interval during which increasing amounts of the expanding bank's notes would nevertheless be presented for settlement at the clearinghouse.

Furthermore, Longfield's argument considers only the *public's* demand for redemption of notes. It overlooks the incentive each bank has to demand redemption of other banks' notes as it receives them from depositors or from borrowers repaying loans. In a competitive system, no bank will pay out the notes of rival banks over its own counter. It will return them to their issuers through the clearing process. If one bank expands out of step with the rest, balances at the clearinghouse will go against it, and it will lose gold paid to its rivals in settlement. This mechanism would work at an earlier stage than the external drain of gold; the bank would begin to suffer reserve drain almost immediately (a point stressed by Lawrence White and George Selgin, cited below). This effect comes in addition to the immediate arithmetical reduction in the ratio of reserves to the bank's expanded note issue.

Smith's discussion brings to mind one distinction between two kinds of money, bank notes and checking accounts. Passively and at least temporarily, the ordinary transactions of a member of the public will thrust onto him notes issued by banks besides his own. The same is not true of checking accounts. He will promptly deposit or cash any checks received, which will quickly be routed for payment to the banks they are drawn on.

If money consisted exclusively of checking accounts (with gold bullion, perhaps, serving as the reserve and redemption medium) and if all payments were made by check, the clearing process would operate in the tightest conceivable way. Unlike some portion of bank notes, substantially all checks would be promptly presented for settlement; and any bank expanding its business out of step with the demand for deposits in it would be promptly punished and restrained by adverse clearing balances.

The coexistence of bank notes with bank accounts, then, somewhat dilutes or delays the discipline of the clearing process. Not all notes return quickly to their issuers for redemption. Surely, though, notes relax the discipline only slightly. In an economy with free banking but operating in other respects as it does today, most money would continue to consist of checking accounts. Retail merchants would continue routinely depositing their cash receipts in their own particular banks, each of which would have an incentive to send notes of other banks through the clearing process.

One of the leading issues of monetary assessment and reform concerns the monetary standard. This was clearly implicit in Smith's work and has in recent years been the major starting point for the revival of interest in the question of free banking.

Many questions suggest themselves: How should the money unit be defined? Should the dollar be defined in gold, with all other kinds of money directly or indirectly redeemable in gold? Should the unit be the dollar of government fiat money, with the money supply managed by the central bank under instructions to keep the price level stable? Similarly, what should the base or dominant money be—the kind of money in which other kinds are denominated and ultimately redeemable? (Federal Reserve notes fill this role in the United States nowadays.) Is it necessary to have any base money at all—and any central bank to issue and manage it?

Nobel laureate F. A. Hayek (1976, 1978, 1984) has proposed authorizing the issue of competing private currencies. Ideas linked with his supervision of Smith's dissertation presumably have influenced him. Books by Lawrence White (1984) and George Selgin (1988) survey the history and theory of free banking and propose freedom of banks to issue notes as well as deposits, which would probably be denominated and redeemable either in gold ˙or in government base money, whose amount would have been frozen. The seventh annual monetary conference of the Cato Institute, held in Washington, D.C., in February 1989, was devoted almost entirely to ideas for radical monetary reform along private-enterprise lines; and a book of papers from earlier conferences (Dorn and Schwartz 1987) contains much discussion of similar themes.

An idea that seems promising to Robert Greenfield and me (1983, 1989) would bar the government from issuing money or exerting any special control over the money and banking system. But the government might define a new unit of account in which prices are quoted, contracts written, accounts kept, and so forth, to replace today's unsatisfactory unit, which is the dollar bill of government fiat money. The government would promote the new unit by employing it in its own operations. The unit might be defined by a specific quantity of gold. Because of gold's probable instability in value, however, a unit defined by some comprehensive bundle of goods and services would possess a more nearly stable purchasing power over goods and services in general.

With the government barred from money issue, banks would be free to issue notes and deposits denominated in this new unit. Each bank, faced with competition, would have to keep its notes and deposits redeemable. Redemption would probably take place not in the actual goods and services defining the unit but *indirectly* instead, in equal-valued amounts of some convenient medium, possibly gold but probably designated securities. Routine interbank settlements at the clearinghouse, as well as arbitrage, would quickly reverse incipient deviations of the price level from what corresponded to the unit's commodity-bundle definition. The ordinary member of the public would need to understand the system's details no more than he needs currently to understand Federal Reserve operations.

Far from involving the textbook inconveniences of barter, the proposed system would feature a well-defined unit of account. Freed from the restraints that nowadays seem necessary to maintain, more or less, the value of the government fiat dollar, financial innovation would flourish, bringing a payments system more convenient than the one we know today. Market forces would make the quantity of money accommodate itself to the demand for money at the stable price level corresponding to the unit's definition. This self-regulation of the money supply would bring decisive advantages in macroeconomic performance.

Here is not the place for a full analysis of these issues. My point is that academic discussion of radical, private enterprise–oriented monetary ideas has become respectable again. Public discussion and political feasibility may follow in time. Vera Smith's scholarly review and judicious assessments of the experience and theory that bear on the issues of free banking and central banking should play a prominent role in the ongoing discussions.

Leland B. Yeager
Ludwig von Mises Distinguished Professor of Economics
Auburn University

References

Dorn, James A., and Anna J. Schwartz, editors, *The Search for Stable Money*, University of Chicago Press, Chicago, 1987.

Ente per gli Studi Monetari, Bancari e Finanziari "Luigi Einaudi," *Moneta, Dualismo e Pianificazione nel Pensiero di Vera C. Lutz*, Società Editrice il Mulino, Bologna, 1984.

Greenfield, Robert L., and Leland B. Yeager, "A Laissez-Faire Approach to Monetary Stability," *Journal of Money, Credit, and Banking*, 15:302–315, August 1983.

Gusman, Rosaria Giuliani, "Note Bio-bibliografiche (1912–1976)," in *Ente . . . Einaudi*, 1984, pp. 89–110.

Haberler, Gottfried, "Vera e Friedrich Lutz. Una famosa coppia di economisti dei nostri tempi," in *Ente . . . Einaudi*, 1984, pp. 47–53.

Hayek, Friedrich A., *Choice in Currency*, Institute of Economic Affairs, Occasional Paper 48, London, 1976.

Hayek, Friedrich A., *Denationalisation of Money*, 2d ed., Institute of Economic Affairs, London, 1978.

Hayek, Friedrich A., "The Future Monetary Unit of Value," in Barry N. Siegel, editor, *Money in Crisis*, Pacific Institute for Public Policy Research, San Francisco, and Ballinger Publishing Company, Cambridge, Mass., 1984.

Schwartz, Anna J., "Banking School, Currency School, Free Banking School," *The New Palgrave, A Dictionary of Economics*, Stockton Press, New York, 1987, vol. 1, pp. 182–185.

Selgin, George, *The Theory of Free Banking*, Rowman & Littlefield, Totowa, N.J., 1988.

Veit-Bachmann, Verena, "Friedrich August Lutz," *Neue Deutsche Biographie*, 1987, vol. 15, pp. 565–567.

White, Lawrence H., *Free Banking in Britain*, Cambridge University Press, New York, 1984.

Yeager, Leland B., and Robert L. Greenfield, "Can Monetary Disequilibrium Be Eliminated?" *Cato Journal*, 9, Fall 1989.

Publisher's Note

The publisher would like to thank Mrs. Brenda K. Fowler and Mr. A. Wilson-Smith for their help in bringing their sister's book back into print. Their assistance has been invaluable.

The Rationale of Central Banking was originally published in 1936 by P. S. King and Son in London. We have added the subtitle *and the Free Banking Alternative* to more adequately reflect the breadth and spirit of the work.

For this Liberty*Press* edition, we have newly set the type. Obvious spelling errors have been silently corrected. Footnotes are now numbered consecutively within each chapter. Otherwise, the text and the footnotes have been retained and styled as they were in the original. The bibliography, however, has been significantly enhanced. Citations in the original edition included only last name, title, and year. We have provided full bibliographic information. For their assistance in providing this information on American, English, French, German, and Italian titles, we would like to thank the following scholars: Professor Lawrence White of the University of Georgia, Professor Philippe Nataf of the University of Paris, and Dr. Reinhold Veit and Mrs. Wendula v. Klinckowstroem of the Walter Eucken Institut. A new, full index has been prepared for this edition.

Foreword

[to the Original Edition]

This essay is a study of the historical and analytical bases of the development of Central Banking, the reasons why the note issue was made the exception to the general application of *laissez-faire* principles, and why Central Banking was adopted in preference to "Free Banking" with competition in the note issue.

It has been submitted and approved as a thesis for the Degree of Doctor of Philosophy in the University of London.

My grateful thanks are due to Professor F. A. von Hayek, who first suggested the topic as a subject worthy of research and gave me valuable advice on many occasions. I should like also to acknowledge the assistance given me by the British Library of Political and Economic Science in obtaining some of the less easily accessible material.

London
October 1935

Vera C. Smith

THE
RATIONALE
OF CENTRAL
BANKING

CHAPTER I

Introduction

In the present century centralised banking systems have come to be regarded as the usual concomitant, if not one of the conditions of the attainment of an advanced stage of economic development. The belief in the desirability of central bank organisation is universal. Recently also there have been attempts to widen the unit of control in the movement towards international banking institutions and international co-operation between the already existing central banks of the separate countries. There is, however, a noticeable lack of any systematic examination of the bases of the alleged superiority of centralised banking over its alternative.

Practically all the discussion on the relative merits of a centralised monopolistic banking system and a system of competitive banks all possessing equal rights to trade, took place in a period of some forty to fifty years in the nineteenth century, since when it has never been reopened. In that period, however, the subject was one of the most keenly debated of its time. This is especially true of France, and indeed the period of about twenty years during which French thinkers occupied themselves with this problem is perhaps the most productive of any in French economic literature, both from the point of view of output and from the standpoint of its quality in comparison with that of other countries in the same years.

In the twentieth century most countries have finally decided in favour of a central banking system, but in the nineteenth century (at least up to 1875), again, most especially on the Continent and in the United States—in England the system as it stood after the passage of the Bank Act of 1844 was not seriously challenged after that date—it was still a matter of dispute as to what sort of form the banking system should take. It is notable that when *laisser-faire* theories and politics were at their height so far as other industries were concerned, banking was already regarded as in another category. Even the most doctrinaire free-traders, with the possible exception of Courcelle-Seneuil in France, were unwilling to apply their principles to the business of banking. It was widely contended that banking must be the subject of some special regulations, although what precise form these regulations should take remained an open question for several decades.

Very little attention has been paid in modern economic literature to the consideration of the rationale of the particular system of banking that we have succeeded in evolving, in the light of the progress that has been made in economic science since the time when the problem was in the forefront of discussion.[1] The actual discussion which did take place is, moreover, one of the controversies among our forefathers with which this generation, more especially in England, is surprisingly unfamiliar. Neither do we find that the authorities responsible for introducing central banks into countries previously without them have any clear idea of the benefits to be obtained therefrom.

It is the purpose of this essay to investigate the motives that have in the past led to the establishment of central banks and to discover the theoretical foundations underlying such motives. An examination of the reasons for the eventual decision in favour of a central banking as opposed to a free banking system reveals in most countries a combi-

---

[1] The only recent challenge is that made by Mises in his "Geldwertstabilisierung und Konjunkturpolitik," 1928.

nation of political motives and historical accident which played a much more important part than any well-considered economic principle.

The exact significance to be attached to the terms "free banking" and "central banking" will become clear in the course of the argument, but for the present we shall summarise the problem in the following questions: Is it preferable that the note issue should be in the hands of one single bank, or at any rate a definitely limited number of banks specially authorised to undertake it, and among which one bank holds a position of sufficient predominance over the rest as to be able to exercise some control over them, *or* is it preferable that there should be as many banks of issue as find it profitable to enter the note-issuing business? Further, if this latter alternative is affirmed and plurality is allowed, is it necessary to impose special requirements, such as a prior lien on assets or the deposit of bonds, to protect note-holders from the consequences of bank failures? Secondly, even if the issue of notes is restricted to a single bank, should there not be freedom for the foundation of banks of deposit exercising no rights of issue? The question may be put still more generally: Is it necessary in the interests of sound banking and a stable currency to impose special restrictions, other than those imposed on all business corporations under the company law, firstly, on banks issuing notes, and, secondly, even providing the answer to this is in the affirmative, on banks of deposit which issue no notes?

This was the historical approach to the question as it presented itself to the writers of last century. The place of primary importance was given to the first problem of the note issue, and it is to this that we shall devote most attention. Our plan will be first to sketch the decisive events, relevant to our main topic, in the history of banking and credit in the leading countries, and then to examine the arguments of both sides in the theoretical controversy.

So far as English banking is concerned, the broad outlines were quite clearly drawn at a comparatively early date, and the system, once established, was never very seriously threatened. Scotland is of particular interest, because the Scotch system was quoted by practically every member of the free-banking school as the conclusive example of the remarkably successful functioning of the system they advocated. The United States of America were likewise cited by the protagonists of the central banking school as the clearest *disproof* of the practicability of any such system. France was rather later than England in finally and irrevocably adopting a centralised banking system. Germany went through a series of moves and countermoves before at last deciding in favour of the same plan in 1875, but here it rather distorts the discussion to consider Germany as a whole, and it is more appropriate to consider the separate States, since Germany did not form a unit till 1871. The theoretical discussion of the subject was practically closed by 1875, by which time the question of the standard had come to assume a far greater importance, but in America several points of interest were raised some years later in the debates preliminary to the establishment of the Federal Reserve System.

In our study of the chronological development of the banking systems of England, Scotland, France, the United States and Germany, our main emphasis will be concentrated on those facts, firstly, which mark the choice at various stages between monopoly and competition, and, secondly, which refer to other aspects of Government management and interference in banking in general.

The chief interest of any theoretical treatment of the place of the banking system in the general economy lies in the part it may be assumed to play in the causation of the phenomena of booms and depressions. We shall have occasion to consider some of the theories of trade cycle causation evolved by the disputants in the Free Banking *versus* Central

Banking controversy. Both sides produced evidence to show that financial and industrial crises were not the fault of the particular system they advocated. The most satisfactory theory yet offered in explanation of booms and depressions, however, is one which at that time was undeveloped and which finds the perpetually disequilibrating force in monetary disturbances expressing themselves in a divergence between the "natural" and market rates of interest and between voluntary savings and real investment. This divergence is in some way connected with bank policy, and the question then arises: How can banks continually act as disequilibrating forces? It might be supposed that if banks made mistakes as a result of which they sooner or later found themselves in difficulties, they would in future act differently on the basis of their revised estimates of their opportunities. Such we should expect to be the consequences, provided the banks had to submit to the full effects of their acts. One of the questions which must be put is whether this responsibility condition is not too often shelved by certain features of the particular system of banking organisation which has been favoured by the modern world. While recognising that the maladjustments may be due, not to the specific form of the banking system, but rather to at present unresolved technical difficulties, common to any system, in maintaining equilibrium between savings and investment, or in stabilising the effective quantity of circulating media, it seems not improbable that the tendencies to misdirection are magnified by the form of the system, in particular that part of it which entrusts the determination of the volume of credit to a single authority, between which and the Government there exist reciprocal incentives to paternalism. It is not unlikely that the bolstering up of banking systems by their Governments is a factor which makes for instability.

CHAPTER II

The Development
of Central Banking
in England

It must have been generally true that, chronologically, deposit banking preceded the issue of notes. At least this was so in England and in the early banks at Hamburg and Amsterdam. But banking in general only became important with the development of the issue of notes. People would deposit coin and bullion with a banker more readily when they received something in exchange such as a bank-note, originally in the form of a mere receipt, which could be passed from hand to hand. And it was only after the bankers had won the public over to confidence in the banks by circulating their notes that the public was persuaded to leave large sums on deposit on the security of a mere book-entry. Moreover, bankers could only lend out any great part of what was deposited with them if they could pay out notes in case depositors should suddenly want more cash. And so it was that when the advantages of deposit banking first came to be generally recognised, the most rapid strides were made by those countries where the use of bank currency had been most widespread.

It was in note issuing, then, that the earliest banking problems arose, and it was here that Governments threatened most strongly to establish monopolies under the system of concession by charter. When banking was in its infancy, doubtless many mistakes were made,[1] and there was some justification for a Government's interfering at least to prevent fraudulent operations. And it is very relevant here to point out that when banking was making its first experiments, industry and trade were only just being weaned from mediaeval protectionism, and it took at least a century for the new system to organise a commercial code for large-scale enterprise. The practical non-existence of company law in general before the nineteenth century was especially serious in spheres touching the currency of a country: what damage could be done was likely to have particularly widespread effects, since the whole population dealt in money. But it must be admitted that it is almost certain that by far the most powerful reason leading to the maintenance of Government intervention in the banking sphere, at a time when it was on the decline in other industries, was that power over the issue of paper money, whether such power is direct or indirect, is an exceedingly welcome weapon in the armoury of State finance.

As deposit banking became, from about the 'thirties of last century onwards, more important relatively to the issue of notes, the dispute that had arisen about monopolies in the note-issuing business tended correspondingly to diminish in importance, although it could not fall entirely out of the discussion because of the intimate connection between the two branches of the banking business. Deposits must always have at the back of them a sufficient reserve of currency, and therefore the total amount of currency must be a major factor in the determination of the total volume of deposits that can be created through the lending operations of the banks. Thus, if a central banking authority controls the issue

---

[1] Under complete freedom good banking depends not only on the ability of the bankers, but also on the public's having sufficient knowledge and experience to detect the good from the bad, the genuine from the fraudulent.

of notes, it also controls, though less rigidly, the volume of credit.

Assuming that a paper currency is a desirable adjunct to a country's commercial development, we may conceive three alternative ways in which its issue may be undertaken:

a) It may be subject to the exclusive control of the State;
b) It may be delegated to the control of a single private institution;
c) It may be left to the free competition of a large number of banks of issue.

The system of a single private institution may take various forms. It may be entirely independent of the State, or the latter may exercise control over it either by taking a share in its capital and thus enforcing its will through its representatives on the directorate, or by subjecting it to the dictates, in matters of general policy, of a Minister of Finance. Even when the system is nominally free from State control, however, history shows that virtually such a right will be very difficult for the bank to maintain.

Also the plural system may vary in the nature of the legal framework within which it functions. There have been advocates of a free system who have favoured certain special regulations; others have assumed that the general clauses of a well-devised company law would be sufficient.

Again we should distinguish the case where a single controlling institution has an absolute monopoly from the case where it is the centre of a so-called mixed system in which it certainly holds the major power, but in which its monopoly is to some extent qualified by the existence of a number of other institutions exercising some of the same functions inside narrower limitations.

We can roughly summarise the course of events and swings of policy in the evolution of banks of issue before 1875 under four phases. The first was a preliminary period when banks were only just beginning to emerge, and they were theoretically at liberty to form freely even if it was only because they were not yet obtrusive enough to catch the eye of the legislative authority. In the second period, monopoly, either absolute or to some extent qualified, was dominant. The third phase was characterised by plurality and increasing liberty, but by no means complete freedom. The fourth witnesses the return to restrictions and monopoly, either absolute or along the lines of a mixed system, with centralisation of control.

This scheme is more or less representative, with differences as to dates, of the course of events in England, France and Prussia. Scotland and America fall outside it.

Let us now turn to the more detailed account of the historical facts of banking development that are relevant to our topic. We commence with England, which produced what later became a model for many other countries.

The origins of banking in the modern sense are to be found in about the middle of the seventeenth century, when merchants took to depositing their balances of coin and bullion with the goldsmiths. The goldsmiths then began offering interest on deposits, since they could re-lend them at higher rates, and the receipts they gave in acknowledgment of the deposits began to circulate as money. There thus arose a number of small private firms, all having equal rights, and carrying on the issue of notes unrestricted and free from Government control.

The second period in English banking, dating from the foundation of the Bank of England in 1694, was ushered in by an event of a rather fortuitous political nature. Charles II had had to rely to a very large extent for his financial needs on loans from the London bankers. He ran heavily into debt and in 1672 suspended Exchequer payments and therefore the repayment of bankers' advances. The King's credit was thereby ruined for several decades to come, and it was to provide a substitute for the sources of accommodation thus destroyed that William III and his Government fell in with the scheme of a financier by the name of Patterson for the foundation of an institution to be known as the Governor and Company of the Bank of England. Its establishment was described by the Tunnage Act, among the many clauses of which its incorporation looked an absurdly minor event, as being "for the better raising and paying into the Exchequer of the sum of £1,200,000."

The early history of the Bank was a series of exchanges of favours between a needy Government and an accommodating corporation. In the first instance, the Bank was founded with a capital amounting to £1,200,000. This same sum was immediately lent to the Government and in return the Bank was authorised to issue notes to the same amount.[2] This sudden issue of so many notes produced all the usual accompaniments of a currency inflation. In 1697 the Government renewed and extended the privileges of the Bank, allowing it to increase its capital and therefore its note issue, and also giving it the monopoly of the possession of the Government balances by ordering that henceforth all sums due to the Government must be paid through the Bank, a provision that added considerably to its prestige. Further, it was also provided that no other bank should ever establish itself by the method of acquiring a special Act of Parliament. Lastly, the Act stated that no act of the Governor and Company of the Bank of England was to subject or make liable to forfeiture the particular private and personal property of any member of the corporation, a clause which bestowed on it the privilege of limited liability. This was a favour which was to be denied to all other banking associations for another one and a half centuries.

It was just about this time that the new type of business

_____

[2] In practice the liabilities on note issue were not restricted to this amount. See Feavearyear, "The Pound Sterling," p. 118.

entity known as the joint stock company was taking hold, and it was therefore an obvious step in the reinforcement of the Bank's already privileged position to endow it with some sort of monopoly in this particular type of organisation, which was in so many respects superior to the old forms of business association. Accordingly, when in 1709 the Bank's charter was renewed, besides allowing it to raise its capital in return for a loan to the Government, the relevant Act specified that no firms of more than six partners might issue notes payable at demand or at any time less than six months. This effectively excluded joint stock firms from the note-issuing business, and, since banking in those days was held to be practically synonymous with note issue, from banking business altogether. More than a century was to pass before the application of the prohibition to banking business other than the issue of notes was to be called into question.

In 1713 the charter was further renewed, again in return for a loan to the Government, and as the resources for the loan were to be obtained by raising additional capital, the Bank gained at the same time the right to an increase in its note issue. The 1742 renewal reaffirmed its privileges of "exclusive banking business," and was again accompanied by the now customary loan transaction, this time a loan without interest. After 1751 the Bank was entrusted with the administration of the National Debt. In return for the 1764 renewal of its charter the Bank paid the Government a fee of £110,000. There was another renewal and another loan in 1781 and the same in 1800. In short, between 1694 and the beginning of the nineteenth century the Treasury had benefited no less than seven times by the successive renewals of the charter of the Bank of England,[3] and this, quite apart from the short-term accommodation given by the Bank in the ordinary course of its daily transactions.

[3] See MacCulloch, "A Treatise on Metallic and Paper Money and Banks," p. 42.

The result of the accumulation of an array of privileges was to give the Bank of England a position of prestige and influence in the financial world such as to cause small private banks to experience difficulties in continuing to compete in the same lines of business, and in London the majority of private note issues had been abandoned by about 1780. A further effect was that the smaller banks began to adopt the practice of keeping balances with the Bank of England, which was thus already beginning to acquire the characteristics of a Central Bank.

The period 1797–1819 is interesting from our point of view, not only because it provides an outstanding example of the force of Government pressure on the Bank, but also because the ultimate consequences of the Government's policy towards the Bank were to add to the latter's influential position in the country's banking system. Soon after the outbreak of the French War, Pitt had to ask for advances from the Bank. Now the Bank Act of 1694 had forbidden it to make advances to the Government without the express authorisation of Parliament. For a long time small amounts had nevertheless been advanced on Treasury Bills made payable at the Bank. The legality of this practice had been regarded as doubtful; so in 1793 the Bank applied to the Government for a Bill indemnifying it against liability for the loans it had made in the past and giving it legal authority to continue such transactions in the future, on the condition, however, that they should be kept below a certain figure. Pitt lost no time in getting the Bill through Parliament, but very usefully neglected to insert the limiting clause, so that the Bank became henceforth virtually compelled to comply with Government requirements to any amount. By 1795 these borrowings had become so excessive as to affect the foreign exchanges and seriously endanger the Bank's reserve position, and the Bank directors appealed to the Government asking Pitt to keep down his demands on the Bank, and at the same time it contracted discounts to private customers. What Pitt did, however, was to take all possible steps to facilitate the Bank's lending to the Government. The old dislike of small notes was thrown to the winds:[4] £5 notes were issued for the first time in 1795, and £1 and £2 notes were issued in 1797 in order to provide small currency in conjunction with another measure of that year, namely, the suspension of the payment in cash of the Bank's notes. This suspension of cash payments was procured by the Government by Act of Parliament in order to meet a critical situation in which the Bank was faced by a "run" at a time when it already had an extremely weak reserve position. The Government's action amounted to a legalisation of the bankruptcy of the Bank, and it created a precedent which led the public in future always to expect the Government to come to the aid of the Bank in difficult circumstances.

We cannot here enter upon a discussion of the contribution of causes other than the Government borrowings, to the Bank's difficulties before 1797. Let it suffice to remark that the expansion of credit that the Bank was forced to undertake under Government pressure must, besides having been itself a cause, also have weakened the Bank's capacity to deal with these other causes, since the method of dealing with an outflow of specie, from whatever cause it arises, must be a contraction of credit.

Throughout the period of the rapid depreciation of the pound after 1800, when there were phenomenal increases in bank credits for war finance, Bank of England notes had for all practical purposes the character of legal tender currency. They were not officially so declared prior to 1812, but since they were taken in all Government payments, and perhaps partly out of patriotic motives, they were usually accepted at par. Finally in 1812 the Government declared

[4] The issue of notes for sums less than £1 had been forbidden in 1775 and the issue of notes for less than £5 in 1777.

them to be legal tender for all payments. These events had important effects on the position of Bank of England notes in the country. The country banks began to look on them as backing for their own note issues, and in many parts of the country they took their place in the local circulation for the first time. Another effect of the war experiences was to give the impetus to the first detailed discussion of banking and currency, ushered in by the report of the Bullion Committee, and continued with unlagging vigour till well over the turn of the half century.

There is no doubt that the release of the Bank from its obligation to pay in cash proved very profitable to it. The Bank's interest in the suspension was stressed by several later observers. Gallatin remarks[5] that its declared dividends rose from 7 percent to 10 percent, besides £13,000,000 of extraordinary profits, and Horn writes[6] that on the morrow of its resumption of cash payments its shares fell 16 percent.

The return to more or less normal conditions in 1819 brought with it, already, a tendency to regard the Bank of England as a regulating institution holding some special position of duty in the currency and credit system of the country, and, indeed, the Bank directors made a representation to Parliament protesting against what they regarded as an attempt to establish a system which would place upon them the responsibility "for supporting the whole National Currency."[7]

Despite the fact that the Bank of England note ceased to be legal tender, the country banks tried to keep their customers to the habit of taking Bank of England notes in lieu of gold, and there was by this time very little gold left in the provinces. The country banks still needed gold to cash their own

[5] "Considerations on the Currency and Banking System of the United States," 1831, p. 47.
[6] "La Liberté des Banques," 1866, p. 301.
[7] See "Parliamentary Papers, Reports from Committees, 1819," Vol. III., Report No. 338.

small notes, since the Bank did not issue notes below £5, but in case of extra strain, the Bank's stock of gold in London had already become practically the sole source of supply. Furthermore, the country banks were coming to expect the Bank to lend to them in times of stress. At such times when the notes of country bankers lost their acceptability, the public showed no hesitation in taking the notes of the Bank of England, and these served just as well as gold coin to meet an internal drain of cash. In the 1825 crisis the Bank was at first hesitant about assisting the country banks, but after a week or so turned round and lent freely to them. It assisted not only with gold but also with the re-issue of the £1 notes that had been in circulation in the restriction period, since £5 notes were unsuitable as everyday currency for small transactions.

The blame for the 1825 crisis was laid on the country banks and their issues of small notes. There were at this time between seven and eight hundred of these banks in existence, and between 1810 and 1825 about one hundred and fifty of them had become bankrupt. There emerged an agitation in favour of allowing joint stock banks, other than the Bank of England, to set up, on the grounds that the present private concerns of not more than six partners were too small to be solid and that joint stock companies would be much stronger and more stable. It was pointed out that not only were small groups of inexperienced traders allowed to go freely into the banking business, but that under the existing law it was *only* these who could do so, and that if concerns with greater financial backing could set up, they would drive out the bad firms. The prime mover in the campaign for joint stock banking was Thomas Joplin, whose pamphlet of 1822[8] called attention to the great success of the Scotch system, and who was later to take a leading part in

---

[8] "The General Principles and Present Practice of Banking in England and Scotland."

the foundation of the National Provincial. The Bank of England opposed the proposals relentlessly and countered them by suggesting that it should set up branches itself in the provinces. Lord Liverpool and his colleagues replied that the proposal of the Bank for establishing branches would not be sufficient to provide for the needs of the country. Incidentally, Liverpool,[9] in trying to persuade the Bank that an improvement in the country circulation would be to its own advantage, hinted at the growing tendency for the Bank of England to become the centre of a single gold reserve, the sole depository for gold in times of favourable exchanges and the sole resort for obtaining it in the opposite circumstances.

The success of this campaign marks the beginning of a third period, a period of increased liberalism in English banking. By the 1826 Act joint stock banks were permitted to establish outside a sixty-five mile radius from London and the Bank of England was authorised to set up branches. The presumed evil of small notes was met by an Act of the same year prohibiting the issue of notes of lower denomination than £5.

By this time it had become obvious that banking business did not consist solely in the issue of notes; nor was this necessarily the main department of banking. Another branch of banking had taken root and was awaiting further development: deposits subject to draft by check were already an important feature of the commercial world. The urgency of the demand for the free right to issue notes therefore subsided into the now more important need for greater freedom in the establishment of deposit banks. It was decided that the charter rights of the Bank did not include any monopoly of deposit banking, and in 1833 the Act for the renewal of the

[9] See his letter to the Governor of the Bank of England (1826), printed by J. Horsley Palmer in his "Causes and Consequences of the Pressure on the Money Market," 1837.

Bank Charter accorded the permission for joint stock banks, not issuing notes payable to bearer on demand, to set up in London. The first bank to set up under the new provisions was the London and Westminster, followed by the London Joint Stock Bank, the Union Bank of London, and the London and County Bank.[10]

The 1833 Act also made Bank of England notes legal tender (except by the Bank) for sums above £5 so long as they should maintain their convertibility.[11] The result of this was to strengthen the tendency towards making the metallic reserve a single reserve system in the hands of the Bank of England. Gold still had to be kept on hand at all ordinary times for making payments below £5, but in times of extra heavy demands, especially in times of panic, the country banks paid out Bank of England notes when their own notes were presented, or their deposits withdrawn, and the ultimate demand for gold fell on the Bank of England. From this it was not a very far or unnatural step for the banks to adopt the practice of keeping the greater part of their reserves in the form of balances at the Bank to which they looked to get Bank notes whenever necessary. In this way the Bank became the holder not only of the *gold* reserve of the whole country, but also of the *banking* (cash) reserve.

Between 1826 and 1836 about a hundred joint stock banks of issue had been founded, and of these about seventy had been formed during the last three years, and it was on these that the opponents of a freer banking system blamed the crises of 1836 and 1839. Criticism came especially from Horsley Palmer, then Governor of the Bank of England,[12] and the

[10] All these banks were at the beginning unlimited liability companies; limited liability was not allowed them before 1858.

[11] It also secured the final abolition of the Usury Laws. The Bank had been exempted from them so far as borrowing was concerned, in 1716, but it was not until 1833 that it was free to charge what rates it thought fit for loans it granted itself.

[12] "The Causes and Consequences of the Pressure on the Money Market," 1837.

question was again raised of the relations between movements in the country bank-note circulation and the Bank of England note circulation. The 1832 Parliamentary Committee[13] had been unable to reach any definite conclusion as to whether or not the country issues usually followed movements in the Bank of England issues. Palmer now contended that prior to 1836 the Bank of England had followed up any tendency to an outflow of specie with a contraction of its circulation, but that what should have been the influence of this policy had been rendered nugatory by the imprudent credit facilities and low money rates occasioned by the issues of the joint stock banks. He claimed that between 1834 and 1836 the issues of the joint stock and private banks in the country had together increased by 25 percent, and that this had led to a continuous export of bullion until the Bank had finally been obliged to raise its discount rate, an event which had caused the stringency on the money market in 1836.

It was also his opinion that banking provision had been adequate under the system of private banks existing prior to 1826, and that in face of this it was dangerous to encourage the formation of additional joint stock banks. He thought the merit of the private banks had been grossly understated. "Nearly eighty private banks suspended their payments in 1825," he says, "yet no stronger proof could be afforded of the really substantial state of the country banks at that time than that a very small proportion (it is believed not ten) proceeded to bankruptcy." Palmer's allegations evoked a somewhat ironic reply from Loyd,[14] who failed, he said, to find in the Bank's accounts sufficient evidence of Palmer's contention that the Bank had, during the years under discussion,

[13] Report of the Committee of Secrecy on the Bank of England Charter," 1831–2.
[14] Reflections suggested by a perusal of Mr. J. Horsley Palmer's pamphlet on the "Causes and Consequences of the Pressure on the Money Market," 1837.

kept its securities constant and contracted its circulation when specie diminished. He found rather that the reverse had been the case, and he very much doubted whether the joint stock banks had the power to extend their issues for any length of time should the Bank of England carry out a "regular, steady and undeviating course of contraction." Loyd was claiming that the central issuer, whose notes were now looked upon as reserve money by the joint stock banks, had both the power and the duty to control the action of those banks, while the Bank directors still refused to accept that responsibility. Loyd and his followers considered at the same time that the indirect power of control of the Bank of England was insufficient because the country note issuers were late in following up contractions by the Bank of England.[15]

Most of the discussion after this time centred round these problems of central bank policy and the effectiveness of the control it had over the total circulation and the necessity or lack of necessity for limiting note issues to a predetermined figure. In England the currency and banking controversy tended to overshadow the wider issues of free banking. The two problems were, of course, not entirely independent, and their interconnections will be considered in a later chapter. All that concerns us here is that it is the final victory of the currency school in 1844 which brings us to our fourth period and the decision, at least in practice, in favour of a central banking single reserve system. It was the 1844 Act which ensured the ultimate monopoly of the note issue in the hands of the Bank of England. It provided in the first instance that the Bank of England's fiduciary issue should be limited to a figure of £14,000,000. The other banks of issue at that time in existence were to be allowed the continuance of

[15] See his "Remarks on the management of the circulation and on the condition and conduct of the Bank of England and the Country Issuers during the year 1839."

the right to issue, but the maximum limit of the issues was fixed in each case at the average figure their issues had reached in the period just preceding the Act, and their rights were to lapse altogether if they amalgamated with, or were absorbed by, another bank, or if they voluntarily renounced their rights, and the Bank of England was to acquire such rights to the extent of two-thirds of the authorised issues of the banks concerned. No new bank could acquire rights of issue.

Horsley Palmer now invoked the position of the Bank as, what Bagehot later christened, the "lender of last resort" as grounds for opposing Peel's Act.[16] It would, he said, put the Bank in a very difficult position for rendering aid to the market in times like 1825, 1836 and 1839. Peel's hope that his measure would render such situations much less likely to occur was, as events proved, to be unfulfilled. The 1847, 1857 and 1866 crises showed the Government always ready, on the only occasions when it was necessary, to exempt the Bank from the provisions of the Bank Act, and the opinion was naturally expressed in some quarters that the clause of the Act, limiting the fiduciary issue of the Bank, was a mere paper provision having no practical application, since the Bank of England could always rely on the Government to legalise a breach of it every time it got into a difficult position. The relations between the Bank and the Government were, in fact, a tradition too long established for either the Bank, or the public, or the Government, to envisage anything other than full Government support to the Bank in time of stress. It had always been a privileged and protected institution, and it was in the interests not only of the Bank but also of the Government that it should remain so.

The Bank directors were extremely loath to recognise the delicacy of the Bank's position in a system which, as the re-

---

[16] See Feavearyear, "The Pound Sterling," p. 256.

sult of a long series of Government manipulations, had made it the controlling element in the country's credit structure. It was the nature of this responsibility that Bagehot was analysing in his "Lombard Street."

Looking at the 1844 Act from our position of superior knowledge of what were to be the features of later banking development, in particular the amalgamations of the last quarter of the nineteenth century, it is impossible to ignore the anomaly of the situation in which this Act left the provincial note-issuing banks. Since they were prohibited from acquiring by purchase or absorption the circulation of other banks of issue, there was a tendency towards the preservation of the smaller banks, even when it would have been more economical for them to combine, because it might happen that the profits to be obtained from the retention of the note issue were estimated to be greater than those to be obtained by joining a larger concern. Secondly, joint stock banks which engaged in the note-issuing business were excluded from the London market and had to pay correspondents to pay out their notes in London. A striking case in point in this respect was the National Provincial Bank. This had been founded, not like the London and Westminster Bank as a London bank without note issue under the 1833 Act, but under the 1825 Act as a joint stock bank issuing notes. Thus, although this bank had a head office in London from which the general administration of all its branches was conducted, it was excluded from carrying on any banking business whatsoever in the metropolis. It was these anomalies that Gladstone sought to remove in the Country Note Issues Bill he introduced in 1865. In return for the removal of the disadvantages mentioned above, those banks choosing to take advantage of its provisions (it was to be a permissive Act only) were to pay a tax of £1 percent on their authorised circulation, and the Government was, besides, to have the right to terminate their issues altogether after a period of fifteen years. Hankey and Goschen got this clause of the Bill amended so as not merely to empower the Government to terminate the issues of such banks after fifteen years but to compel it so to do. It was thus to become an instrument for getting rid of the country circulation altogether, but Gladstone so worded the preamble as not to preclude entirely negotiations for a renewal of the term. The Bill failed to pass, however, and in 1866 the National Provincial, probably the bank most concerned, started a banking business in London at the price of sacrificing its right to issue notes. From this time onwards the joint stock banks concentrated their efforts on deposit business.

The theoretical discussion lingered on a few years longer, largely as the reflection of developments abroad.

CHAPTER III

The
Scottish
System

But for the fact that the Act of Union was just over a decade too late, the Bank of England might have been the Bank of England and Scotland. As it was, however, Scottish banking developed along independent lines. At the beginning, the practice of giving concessions by charter was followed. The Bank of Scotland, founded by a group of Scottish merchants in 1695, only a year after the establishment of the Bank of England, received under Charter from the Scottish Parliament a monopoly for twenty-one years. This Bank experimented almost immediately with a policy of setting up branches, and it also issued notes for denominations as low as £1. When in 1716 the Bank's monopoly expired, it protested strongly against threats of competition, but without success, and in 1727 a second charter was granted to the Royal Bank of Scotland.

The primary object of forming under special charter was that the Bank obtained thereby the right to limited liability, but there was no restriction in Scotland on the liberty of joint stock companies to set up in the banking business so long as the shareholders were willing to accept unlimited liability for the debts of the association, and not much time elapsed before unchartered banks of this kind were starting up all over the country.

Only one further charter was granted: this was to the British Linen Company in 1746. All the other banks formed under the ordinary law. There was no restriction on the number of partners and, after a short period of abuses in the experimental stage, banking came into the hands of a number of substantial joint stock companies of considerable size and financial strength. The collapse of the Ayr Bank in 1772 after an over-issue of notes did a great deal of damage to the credit of the smaller banks; most of the little private banks went out of business and their place was taken by joint stock banks or private banks with larger capital resources.

The Scottish system developed certain characteristics which early distinguished it from the systems in other countries. There was keen competition between the banks and they kept very strictly to the practice of regularly clearing each other's notes; exchanges were made twice a week and the balances immediately settled. They adopted branch organisation almost from the beginning, and there was, as compared with other countries, a much more rapid growth of deposit banking and development of loan technique.

In 1826 there were, besides the three chartered banks (with twenty-four branches), twenty-two joint stock banks (with ninety-seven branches) and eleven private banks, whereas in England legislation was only just being passed to permit joint stock banks to establish, and not even the Bank of England had yet set up any branches. Right up to that time there had only been one serious failure in the history of Scotch banking—the Ayr disaster—and it was computed that the total loss sustained by the public had not exceeded a figure of £36,000.

The Scottish network of solid institutions, free from legislative interference, with an already highly developed deposit business—its marked success and its freedom from the excesses which lead to suspensions—could not help but impress English eyes at a time when large numbers of the small country banks in England were foundering. Still more, perhaps, did it impress the protagonists of free banking on the Continent.

The investigations by Committees of both Houses of Parliament in 1825 into the supposedly evil practice of the issue of £1 notes and the suggestion that it should be prohibited alike in Scotland as in England aroused bitter indignation in Scotland. The Scottish community had become, by long use, accustomed to handling £1 notes instead of gold in their daily transactions, and it was consequently not from the banking interests alone that the protests derived. Notable among the antagonists was Sir Walter Scott. It was, indeed, difficult for the promoters of the 1826 legislation to claim on the experiences of Scotch banking that the issue of £1 notes had had any catastrophic results.

Scotland escaped the censure of its £1 notes, but had to submit to the Peel regulations of 1845. These conferred a monopoly of the note issue on the then existing Scotch banks. The fiduciary issue of each bank was limited to a maximum fixed on the basis of an average taken over the previous year, but, unlike the English banks, the Scotch ones could issue notes above this fixed limit so long as they backed the extra notes a 100 percent by gold, and also if two banks fused they might retain a fiduciary issue equal to the combined issues of both.

The regulation imposed by the Act was regarded with dissatisfaction for many years afterwards. In 1864 complaints were coming from Scottish quarters that owing to bank extinctions Scottish note issues had diminished and Bank of England notes were not fitted to fill the gaps because they were not issued below the denomination of £5. And for the comfort of the opponents of Peel's legislation the next thirty years witnessed two of the worst failures the Scottish banking system had ever experienced, comparable only with that of the Ayr Bank a century before. These were the collapse of the Western Bank in 1857 and of the Glasgow Bank in 1878.

CHAPTER IV

The Development
of Central Banking
in France

$\mathbf{T}$he unfortunate first experiences of note issues in France retarded banking development in that country for many years. The monopoly given to John Law in 1716 for his *Banque Générale* resulted in a disastrous over-issue of paper, and the bank closed after five years. The Government thereafter raised the restrictions on the formation of note-issuing banks, but although firms set up to carry on other branches of banking business, chiefly discounting and exchange transactions, no bank of issue was founded before 1776. This was the *Caisse d'Escompte,* a partnership with limited liability, founded by Turgot, the French Minister of Finance. From the very beginning this bank came into very close relations with the State, and became, in fact, practically a branch of the financial department of the Government. The promise of an advance of 6,000,000 frs. to the Treasury in 1783 caused a "run" on the bank and it suspended payments. The exigencies of the State finances, already heavily in debt to the Caisse, resulted in the giving of forced currency to its notes in 1788, and after this followed the *assignat régime.* The first assignats, issued in 1789, which were not themselves legal tender but short-dated interest-bearing Government bonds, backed by the *biens nationaux,* were usually discounted with the Caisse. But in 1790 the assignats became legal tender currency. France was flooded with them and the Caisse collapsed, leaving behind it a distrust of paper money which was to be widespread and long-lived.

A decree of 1792 had forbidden the establishment of banks of issue, but the abrogation of this decree and the restoration of the ordinary currency in 1796–97 encouraged some of the Paris discount banks to undertake the issue of notes. Chief among these were the *Caisse des Comptes Courants* and the *Caisse d'Escompte du Commerce*. A new development took place in 1798 when a bank of issue was set up in the provinces, namely, at Rouen. This bank took the step of issuing notes as small as 100 frs. The Paris banks had not been in the habit of issuing notes for less than 250 frs. The freedom prevailing at this time in banking in France seems to have proved very satisfactory, and no disasters occurred, but the march of political events destined this state of affairs for a short existence.

Napoleon's mania for centralisation and his difficulty in getting Government paper discounted, chiefly owing to the lack of confidence in that Government, turned his attention to the potentialities of a bank founded under Government auspices. So in 1800 he persuaded the stockholders in the *Caisse des Comptes Courants* to dissolve the company and merge it into a new bank, called the Bank of France. The Bank was financed with an initial capital of 36,000,000 frs., obtained partly from the original capital of the *Caisse des Comptes Courants*, partly by new subscription by the public and partly from Government funds, obtained from the sinking fund of the national debt. Soon after the foundation of the Bank the Government sold out a large part of its shares, but the independence of the Bank was not thereby much increased. Further negotiations, and manipulations, largely quite unscrupulous, were undertaken in 1802, as a final result of which the *Caisse d'Escompte du Commerce* was unwillingly induced to fuse with the Bank of France.

The most severe blow to competition came a year later, however, when the Government, by the famous *loi du 24 Germinal an XI,* granted to the Bank of France the exclusive privilege of issuing notes in Paris, ordered those Paris banks already issuing notes to withdraw them by a certain date, and forbade the organisation of any bank of issue in the provinces except by the consent of the Government, which reserved the right not only to grant all privileges of issue but also to fix the maximum of such issue. The pretext for this piece of legislation was the slight financial crisis in 1802, but, in fact, nobody had brought any accusation against the competitive banks.

From the outset the Bank of France was under continuous pressure from Napoleon. As early as 1804 a dispute arose between them because the Bank was not discounting Government paper cheaply enough. Under this pressure the Bank discounted too much and issued more notes than it had the specie to maintain. This over-issue, together with the spread of a rumour to the effect that Napoleon had sent away the metallic reserves of the Bank to Germany for military needs, saw the Bank in serious difficulties in the following year. It had partially to suspend payment and its notes depreciated 10 percent to 15 percent. For this Napoleon laid the blame on the Bank and determined to bring its constitution more under the Government. So in 1806 he gave the State a larger share in the Bank's administration by replacing the Committee elected by the stockholders by a Governor and two deputy-Governors appointed by the head of the State.

Further heavy loans to the Treasury in 1813 caused another partial suspension of cash payments in the next year. This gave impetus to a good deal of criticism and to a movement of opinion in favour of making the Bank independent of the Government, but nothing came of this proposal.

It soon became apparent that France was extremely backward, as compared with England and America, in the development of banking facilities; particularly slow was the pace at which they grew in the provinces where, so far, and apart from small firms specialising on exchange business, they were practically non-existent. Special authority had been given to the Bank of France in 1808 to set up branches, and in those towns where it established them it was to have exclusive rights of issue. It set up its first branch offices in Lyons, Rouen and Lille, but they were all closed down after a very brief existence, because they had proved unprofitable in the difficult years in which they had begun, and it was also argued in favour of their suppression that their demands might, in periods of tight credit, encroach on the reserve of the central bank in Paris.

Almost immediately on the abandonment by the Bank of France of the attempt to establish credit facilities outside Paris, there was a short period of increasing liberalism, during which three projects were sanctioned by the Government of the Restoration for the establishment of private departmental banks of issue. These were the Banks of Rouen, Nantes and Bordeaux, formed in 1817–18. But these banks were subjected to severe restrictions, which were of a nature to defeat any great expansion of their business. They had the right to issue notes only for their headquarters and one or two other towns mentioned in their statutes; they could only discount bills payable in their own district; and their sight liabilities might not exceed three times the amount of their metallic reserves. The restrictions of their operations to such narrow districts and their inability to set up branches or employ agents almost belied the title "Departmental." Their sphere of operations was infinitely smaller than the *département*, and they were, in fact, merely small local banks. Nevertheless, six additional departmental banks were founded between 1835 and 1838, and the Bank of France, now taking fright at the threat of a competing banking interest, began itself to organise branch offices, fifteen of which were started between 1841 and 1848. Each branch the Bank opened was of course given a monopoly of the note issue in its own town. Moreover, *Comptoirs* of the Bank of France required for their authorisation only an *ordonnance royale*, which would be granted on the recommendation of the *Conseil Générale de la Banque*, whereas departmental banks after 1840 had to obtain a special Act of Parliament. Also the greater area over which the *Comptoir* as a member of a branch system could conduct business gave it a great advantage over the departmental bank. There never even developed among the departmental banks any system of exchange of notes: nevertheless, the success of these banks and the services they rendered to the community were far from insignificant. They met with the disapproval of the Bank of France and after 1840 the Government refused to grant any more charters for their foundation. So the movement towards greater freedom in the note-issuing business was brought to an end. The representations of the departmental banks to the Chamber of Deputies, on the occasion of the discussions of the renewal of the charter of the Bank of France, asking for modifications of their statutes in the direction of removing some of the restrictions they contained, were also unsuccessful.[1]

The trend of policy towards complete centralisation of the note issue reached its logical conclusion as a result of the 1848 political disturbances, but the opposition voiced by the Bank of France to the renewal of the charter of the Bank of Bordeaux in that year makes it practically certain that the

---

[1] Their chief claims were the following: *(a)* to be allowed to discount paper payable not only in their own town, but also in any town having a bank; *(b)* to be able to discount bills having two signatures only, the present requirement being three; *(c)* to be authorised to issue notes for 100 frs.

departmental banks would in any case not have survived after the expiration of their charter rights.

The 1848 political crisis foreshadowed in many people's minds a repetition of the *assignat régime,* and their first instinct was to hoard specie, with the inevitable consequence of a run on the banks. The Government was naturally interested in preserving the capacity of the Bank of France to give it financial support in dealing with the insurgents. It therefore gave to the Bank's notes *cours forcé* and allowed it to issue notes for 100 frs.,[2] at the same time imposing what it regarded as a safeguard against excessive issues by putting a maximum limit of 350,000,000 frs. on its note issue. The departmental banks were, it is true, given what were nominally the same facilities, and their notes subjected to a maximum limit which amounted to 102,000,000 frs. for all nine banks together, but since their notes were made legal tender only within their own respective localities, while the notes of the Bank of France were legal tender all over France, the circulation of the Bank of France gained an overwhelming ascendancy over that of the departmental banks. The 1848 decree was consequently their ruin rather than their salvation, and in the same year they agreed to submit to a fusion with the Bank of France, practically the only course that remained open to them short of liquidation. Thus by two Government decrees they became *Comptoirs* of the Bank of France, which acquired their authorised note issues as an addition to its legal maximum.

The events of the period immediately following 1848 throw light also on the subordination of the Bank to the will of the Treasury. Up to the decree to which we referred above, the Government had never imposed any limitation on

[2] Up till 1847 the Bank had not been allowed to issue notes in Paris for less than 500 frs. At the *Comptoirs* in the provinces it could, like the departmental banks, issue them for as low as 250 frs. In 1847 the same minimum denomination was made to apply to Paris, where provincial notes for that amount had in any case been circulating previously.

the amount of the note issue. It had been content to rely, on the Bank's obligation to pay specie on demand, and on a prohibition of small notes. Now that both these checks were gone, it did, as we have seen, impose a limit, but this the Government showed itself ever ready to raise if it should form any obstacle to the Bank's readiness to lend to the Treasury. The difficulties of the Bank of France in meeting its obligations in cash, which had been the avowed reason for legalising its bankruptcy, had, so far as its private commercial obligations were concerned, been of very short duration, and it showed itself ready at an early date to revert to cash payments. But the scale at which Government borrowings at the Bank continued made its position unstable. In June, 1848, and again in November, 1849, the Government had arrived at agreements with the Bank by which the latter was to make regular advances of fixed sums during the succeeding two or three years. At the end of 1849 the Bank had received permission to increase its issue to 525,000,000 frs. By this time, however, it had a very strong metal reserve (about 400,000,000 frs.), and it had already begun suppressing the restrictive measures relating to the redemption of its notes, and it would probably have decided in favour of a complete resumption of cash payments much earlier if it had not been for the Government borrowing factor. If Treasury demands were going to continue at the same rate, the Bank believed its cash reserve would be inadequate. On the other hand, its note issue very soon approached the new maximum, and the Bank was faced with the choice either of applying for a further increase of its legalised circulation or of reverting to its old statutes under which it would be obliged to redeem its notes and *cours forcé* would be abolished, but there would be no legal limitation on the total volume of notes it was allowed to issue. It was only after an agreement had been reached with the Treasury for the reduction of the Bank's obligations to lend, that the Bank felt safe in reverting to its old statutes, and this it finally did in August, 1850.

We have seen how France emerged from the 1848 political crisis with a completely centralised, single, monopoly bank of issue. The progress of the industrial revolution in France round about 1850 brought into greater prominence the extreme paucity of credit facilities, most especially in the provinces, but even in Paris itself. Where facilities for the spread of a paper circulation had been withheld there was a corresponding absence of deposit banking, and the contrast was particularly strong with England where the country bankers with local connections and knowledge, even if they had rendered no other service, had at least accustomed the timid provincial mind to banking habits. Courcelle-Seneuil, especially, stressed the practical impossibility in the rural districts of France of either borrowing or lending, except through the local *notaire*. Moreover, as he also pointed out,[3] the fact that the farmers received the proceeds of the sales of their crops and stocks in lump sums at a particular time in the year and had to make their disbursements much more slowly over a much longer period meant that they were in possession of balances of spare cash for the greater part of the year. These balances could have been deposited in the banks and used to make short-term loans if there had been local banks to deal with the business. As it was, the balances simply went into hoards, and savings were not used.

We have now described the features which set the stage for the opening of the free-banking controversy in France. In addition, less commendable but nevertheless very powerful grounds were provided by the gradual emergence during the next two decades of the beginnings of a discount policy, the occasional stringency of which evoked a torrent of criticism against the Bank of France. This partic-

---

[3] "La Banque Libre," 1867.

ular aspect of the discussion is explained by a conception of the nature and object of banking which had its origins in the very earliest days of French banking. Right from the beginning the Government had imposed limitations on the flexibility of discount rate. In the case of the *Caisse d'Escompte* it was forbidden to charge more than 4 percent. The rate of discount of the Bank of France was fixed provisionally by the Government at 6 percent, and for the first six years it was held invariable at that figure, until in 1806 it was reduced to 5 percent. Discount policy in these years was primarily conditioned by the claims of Napoleon. It was his idea that the aim of the Bank of France must be to discount for all commercial firms of reasonable standing at 4 percent, and he criticised the Bank for not being liberal enough, and it was at his instance that the rate was reduced to 4 percent in 1807. It was not changed again until 1814, when it was raised to 5 percent. It seems to have been the policy of the Bank to maintain as far as possible a *stable* rate, for it was sticky in both directions, and when the Bank found it necessary to extend or to contract credit, it would adopt almost any conceivable means of doing so other than that of adjusting[4] the price it charged for its loans. In 1819 it adopted for some months the policy of charging a lower rate (4 percent) on bills of short date (having less than thirty days to run) before it finally decided to reduce all rates to 4 percent. In times of strain it kept the rate of interest constant and resorted to rationing, or to the purchase of specie at a premium, in order to strengthen its reserve. It was for the first time in

[4] In times of strain it always meant that some form of rationing had to be resorted to. M. Rouland, Governor of the Bank of France, remarked before the Commission of Enquiry (1865) that when the Bank kept its rate of discount fixed it often had to reject demands for discounting at that rate in considerable proportions. So he states that in 1812, 30 percent of the total demands were rejected, in 1832, 14 percent and in 1841 and 1842, 6 percent. See "Dépositions de MM. les délégués et les régents de la Banque de France," p. 116.

1847 that it discovered the effectiveness of a rise in the rate in stemming a drain of cash. It had already relowered its rate when the 1848 crisis brought another shock, and it was still too much afraid of using the weapon of discount rate to combat it. It continued throughout the year to discount at 4 percent, while the departmental banks, which were less able to bear the strain, were charging 6 percent. The reduction of the rate in 1852 to 3 percent brought to an end a period of just over thirty years, during which, with the sole exception of 1847, its rate of discount had remained unchanged at 4 percent. This is in striking contrast to the practice of the Bank of England, whose rate was changed no less than fifty times between September, 1844, and December, 1856.

From the 'fifties onwards the French rate began, however, to fluctuate more frequently. The greater willingness to change the rate was probably strengthened by the greater need to do so, arising with the increased mobility of specie due to improved transport facilities and communications, which made arbitrage operations much easier. Also, perhaps, some allowance should be made for the beginnings of the activities of the *Crédit Mobilier* in the direction of capital export. Anyhow, a strong tendency to an outflow of specie set in between 1855 and 1857, culminating with the crisis of that year. The Bank was at first hesitant about raising bank rate, and in the autumn of 1856 the Governor asked the Emperor to sanction a suspension of cash payments. This the Emperor refused and the Bank next reverted to the practice of imposing a limit (two months) on the *échéance* of bills it was prepared to discount. Finally in 1857 it gave definite recognition to the principle of raising bank rate when there is a drain on the specie reserve, and in that year the Usury Laws prohibiting a rate above 6 percent were abrogated so far as the Bank of France was concerned. But even so, the Bank still relied partly on the method of charging higher rates on the longer-dated bills. In 1861 the rate was held for some weeks at 7 percent, and from that time onwards it fluctuated much more violently than heretofore, and began to oscillate more or less in harmony with the Bank of England rate.

In England the doctrine of bank rate was now fairly generally accepted, largely owing to the writings of MacLeod. But in France it provoked the first big attack on the Bank, and a corresponding demand in some quarters for permission to establish other banks of issue. Many of the adherents of this view pointed out that the charter by which the Bank of France was granted its privilege did not prevent the establishment in France of other banks of issue, that it was a monopoly not by law but in fact only, and that the Government was free to give rights to other institutions in places not occupied by the Bank.

Increased practical significance was given to the discussion by incidents arising out of the annexation of Savoy in 1864, and it was around the Bank of Savoy controversy that the more general question came to be focussed. Not the least disinterested and perhaps the most prominent among the participants in the discussion were the Pereire brothers, founders of the new type of credit institution known as the *Crédit Mobilier*. This was a bank which carried out underwriting, the marketing of bonds and equities, and even direct subscription to the newly issued capital of industrial companies, as well as to State loans. The founders had projects for setting up similar institutions in other countries. This they failed to do directly, although the French *Crédit Mobilier* was imitated independently in Germany. The Pereire brothers had from the outset always hoped to add to their other financial business the business of note issue; this was incidentally a combination that had exceedingly little chance of success, as was proved by German experiences. Investments which consist for the most part of industrial securities and which are difficult to sell in certain states of the market except at heavy loss prove very dangerous assets to hold against liabilities of the very shortest term, viz., notes payable on demand. The Pereires, however, saw no possibility of obtaining note-issuing rights until the rights of the Bank of Savoy came up for discussion and reopened the whole question of free trade in banking *versus* the monopoly of the Bank of France.

The treaties accompanying the annexation of Savoy established that individuals and institutions belonging to Savoy should be allowed to exercise the same rights in France as they had held under the law of Savoy, and the Bank of Savoy concluded from this that it had the right to establish branches over the whole of France and to issue notes payable on demand. It was here that the *Crédit Mobilier* saw its chance. It concluded an agreement with the Bank of Savoy by which the Pereires were, by their own subscription, to raise a capital of the bank to ten times its present amount and gain a controlling influence in the concern. The Bank of France was much alarmed at the prospect of having the Bank of Savoy as a competitor, especially as certain features of the Bank of Savoy's business were likely to make it a keen rival. The Bank of Savoy paid interest to depositors, issued notes for as low a denomination as 20 frs., and could discount two-named paper, whereas the Bank of France paid no interest on deposits and had not as yet issued notes for less than 100 frs.,[5] and could only discount three-named bills. The Bank of France made a protest on the plea of the Government's contractual obligation to maintain its privilege, and obtained from the Minister of Finance a letter signifying the Government's opposition to the Pereire agreement with the Bank of Savoy, and then entered itself into negotia-

[5] At the renewal of its charter in 1857 it had acquired the right to issue notes for 50 frs. It actually first took advantage of this in 1864, at the time of the Bank of Savoy affair.

tions with that Bank, as a consequence of which the latter agreed to renounce its claims to issue notes in return for an indemnity.

This incident, together with the raising of the discount rate to 8 percent in 1864, directed the attention of many people to the hitherto rather neglected subject of the theory of the money market. Its immediate effect was to produce a demand for the appointment of a Commission to enquire into the policy of the Bank of France. Isaac Pereire wrote a pamphlet demanding such an enquiry, and the Emperor received a petition from 300 Paris merchants also demanding an investigation, on the grounds that the raising of the discount rate by the Bank of France had led to the periodic return of crises. Finally the Bank itself suggested that these demands should be satisfied, so that its position, in face of the attacks that were being made against it, might be elucidated.

The direction of the enquiry was undertaken by the *Conseil Supérieur du Commerce de l'Agriculture et de l'Industrie*. The discussions opened in February, 1865, and did not finish until June, 1866, by which time much of the earlier enthusiasm had died down. The problems raised for discussion were primarily two: firstly, whether the Bank's new policy of raising its discount rate in times of strain was preferable to its old policy of maintaining its rate invariable, and, secondly, whether a single bank of issue was superior to a plural system of competing banks. Evidence was taken from practically all those having any competence to speak on the subject. The results showed a verdict of the majority on both issues in favour of the Bank of France.

This may be taken to mark the close of the discussion so far as the practical issue was concerned, but among the more academic writers it continued for several years longer, until it was superseded at the beginning of the 'seventies by the bimetallic question. It was a strange coincidence that the

Crédit Mobilier, the chief engineer of the accusation against the Bank of France, should almost at the very moment of the Bank's acquittal find itself in serious difficulties, which were to lead to its going into liquidation only a year later.

At the same time as France was consolidating her centralised system, the trend in neighbouring countries was in the same direction. In Holland the debates in 1863 on the proposal to replace the monopoly of the Netherlands Bank by free trade in the issue of notes had resulted in a decision in favour of the retention of the monopoly. In Italy increased centralisation of the note issue was proceeding *pari passu* with political unification.

CHAPTER V

The Organisation
of Banking in America:
Decentralisation
Without Freedom

The Scottish experiences served as a forceful example in support of the claims of the free-banking school, but appeals to American history can hardly be said to have been so fortunate. The American case was evoked as evidence by both sides in the controversy, but so far as the system as a whole is concerned, it cannot be described as an illustration for either. It was decentralised without freedom; it lacked the essential characteristics both of central banking and of free banking proper.

The distribution of powers between the Federal and the State authorities left legislative control in banking matters in the hands of both. The country started off with a natural dislike of centralised institutions and a jealous regard for individual State rights. Nevertheless, the need for funds in the War of Independence impelled the Federal Government to take the first initiative in the banking sphere in the promotion of the Bank of North America. The lack of a genuine commercial need for banking facilities at this very early period in America's industrial development caused great difficulty in getting private capital for such an enterprise, and the Government was obliged to become a substantial shareholder in the Bank. It shared the unpopularity of all central institutions, and after the war its charter was repealed.

Not very long afterwards banks began to set up in the more progressive States under the separate legal systems of the various States concerned. The usual procedure at the beginning was to apply for a charter which gave the bank the privilege of limited liability. In most cases the charter contained clauses limiting the amount of liabilities the banks might legally incur to a certain multiple of their paid-up capital,[1] and in some instances it imposed also a lower limit on the denomination of notes. In very few States did unchartered banks set up with unlimited liability.[2] Almost as soon as any possibility arose of private individuals and unincorporated associations wanting to set up without charter, restrictions were placed on their entry into the banking business by the legislatures concerned. Most of the eastern States passed laws similar to the 1818 law of New York, which made both deposit banking and note issue conditional on special legal authorisation, and the majority of the Western States followed up the same policy. But the actual effect of this rule varied from State to State according to the ease with which charters were obtainable. There was least stringency in the east, which was, of course, the district in which there was most call for banking facilities. The most liberal policy was to be found in New England and more especially in Massachusetts and Rhode Island, where charters were granted to nearly all

[1] The most common rule was that note issues should not exceed double the amount of the bank's capital. Such provisions were, however, usually purely nominal; the limits they imposed were never likely to be reached. See Gallatin, "Considerations on the Currency and Banking System of the United States," 1831, p. 65.

[2] Only in England and Scotland were joint stock companies generally subjected to unlimited liability. In America, as well as on the Continent, the principle of limited liability became the general rule right from the beginning.

who applied for them.[3] In New York already established banks seem to have exercised a powerful influence in persuading the legislature to refuse to grant charters to new competitors; and there was an increasing tendency to restriction the further you went south and west.

Meanwhile, a second attempt had been made to run a central bank. This was the Federal institution, known as the First Bank of the United States.[4] From its parent bank at Philadelphia the company had early begun to develop branches, and this caused much annoyance to the State banks and their legislatures. The opposition of the Republican Party was forceful enough to secure its suppression when its charter came up for renewal in 1811.

The disappearance of this bank and its branches was followed by a rapid growth of State banks. In 1811 there had been about eighty-eight, and within the next three years a hundred and twenty new bank charters were granted. Most of these banks lent heavily to the Federal Government when war was declared in 1812, and their excessive issues caused about three-quarters of them[5] to seek the sanction of their respective Governments to suspensions of cash payments in 1814. After this their issues expanded still further and their notes fell to discounts ranging from 10 to 30 percent.[6] The

[3] See Carey, "The Credit System of France, Great Britain and the United States," 1838, p. 68.

[4] Founded in 1791. The Federal Government had subscribed part of the capital and pledged itself not to grant a charter to any other bank for the next twenty years.

[5] The New England banks fulfilled their engagements. All the banks to the south and west failed. See Gallatin, "Considerations on the Currency and Banking System of the United States," p. 42. Most failures in these and the following years took place where entry into the banking trade was most restricted. Carey gives figures of failures from 1811 to 1830. In New England as a whole the number of banks between 1811 and 1830 averaged 97 and the total failures were 16. In New York the banks averaged 26 and there were 11 failures. In Pennsylvania there were 29 banks with 19 failures, and the proportion of loss increases as you go further to the west and south.

[6] Gallatin estimated that within the first fifteen months of the suspension of specie payments, their note issues increased by 50 percent. *Op. cit.*, p. 45.

resumption of specie payments nominally took place in 1817, but in 1819 there was a further suspension, which lasted two more years.

The foundation of these early banks was much more often based on political influence than on real commercial necessity. It was attended by abuses in the paying in of capital which were often directly aided by the State. In the case of the First Bank of the United States itself, the United States Government subscription of $200,000,000 was a purely fictitious book entry. Some of the banks had scarcely any capital at all, and nearly all of them had much less than was nominally subscribed, and since the liability of shareholders was limited, there was very little protection for the creditors. The State legislatures, when they did at last set themselves the task of opposing these fraudulent practices, experienced incredible difficulties in framing legislation to deal with them.

Another feature of these early banking formations was their close connection with State Treasuries. It was a common practice for States to require banks to make loans when necessary to the State chartering them. Special provisions were often made for this in their charters, and in addition Acts were passed from time to time authorising specific loans. The result of this frequently was that the banks were so heavily "loaned up" to the Government as to have practically no substance left for supplying commercial demands, a factor which must have contributed considerably to their early excesses.

The result of the autonomy of the rather small sparsely populated area of the State was that the banking system tended to assume a very fragmentary nature. A State bank had rights to carry on business only within the borders of the State from which it received its charter. This meant that America could not develop a branch system of banking, and it was perhaps in this circumstance that the chief justification lay for an institution such as the First Bank of the United

States. Secretary of the Treasury, Gallatin, expressed the opinion some years later that if the Bank of the United States had been in existence in 1814, the chaotic banking disturbances of that year would not have occurred.[7] The most essential condition for the suppression of excess note issues is their presentation for payment at frequent intervals. A very serious trouble throughout the history of American banking was the lack of a regular system of clearing the notes of the various banks. Notes tended to travel considerable distances, and since a bank in one State had no branches in any other State and generally no correspondents either, there existed no ready-made agencies for collecting the notes of rival banks and presenting them for payment. This was a function that the First Bank had begun successfully to perform, and its consequences must undoubtedly have been to curb the tendencies of the local banks to excessive note issues.

Another experiment in centralised banking institutions was made in 1816 with the foundation of the Second Bank of the United States. In common with the First Bank, part of its capital was subscribed by the Government, and it was to be the depository of the balances of the Federal Treasury without obligation to pay interest on them. It had, moreover, the right to establish branches without consulting the Governments of the States concerned. A new feature of its charter was a clause intended to minimise the likelihood of cash suspensions, by imposing a penalty, in the event of its failing to meet its obligations on demand, in the form of a 12 percent tax on the amount in default.

Gallatin maintains that it was only as a result of the organisation of this bank that the State banks were prevailed upon to resume cash payments, since it was the Second Bank which proposed a convention to which the State banks finally agreed. It is interesting to note that one of the stipula-

---

[7] "Considerations on the Currency and Banking System of the United States," p. 46.

tions made by the State banks was that the Bank of the United States should, in any emergency that might menace the credit of any of the said banks, contribute its resources to any reasonable extent in their support. This is a very early declaration of the view that it is the duty of the central bank to act as lender of last resort.

The Second Bank of the United States and its twenty-five branches soon came into conflict with the defenders of State rights, and of course the State banks backed up the opposition. The chief objection brought by the latter against the Bank was that it "accumulated their notes and then presented them for redemption in coin." "War" was declared on the Bank by Jackson when he succeeded to the Presidency in 1829. The first blow was struck in 1833 when he gave orders for the Government deposits to be removed from the Bank and deposited instead in selected State banks. Shortly afterwards the renewal of the Bank's charter was vetoed. This put an end for many decades to all projects for a central bank.

General suspensions of cash payments occurred in 1836, except in New England, where the banks again kept above water. Probably the worst feature of the American system and the one to which, combined with the exclusion of the entry of new firms, much of the chaos was due, was the extreme laxity with which principles of bankruptcy were applied to insolvent banks. Take as an example the State of New York. In charters granted before 1828 there were provisions that if a bank suspended payment for a certain period (usually three months) it should cease operations unless it obtained permission to continue, after an examination of its affairs, from the Chancellor of the Circuit, and if at the end of a year it still did not resume payment, it should surrender its rights altogether. Charters created after 1828 shortened the unconditional period allowed to ten days. But in 1837 all these rules were made completely ineffectual because the

State legislature passed a Suspension Act allowing suspending banks to continue for a year without applying to the Commissioner. Other States followed New York's example and passed Suspension Laws of an even more pernicious nature.[8]

Further suspensions took place in 1839, but were confined this time to Pennsylvania and the States further to the south and west. Boston and the eastern States sustained payments. Pennsylvania passed laws legalising the suspension on condition that the banks should make certain loans of money to the State, and it was arranged that they should resume specie payments in January, 1841. The obligation to lend to the Government naturally had the effect of making it more difficult, if not impossible, for the banks to resume payments, and the date for resumption was postponed by another Act which, in return for further subscription to a Government loan, allowed the banks to continue the suspensions until the loan was repaid, which might be any time up to five years.[9]

The losses sustained by the Federal Treasury in the suspensions of 1836 and 1839 called forth proposals for making the Treasury independent of the banks.

From the 'forties onwards State banking showed signs of improvement. Most of the States had by this time succeeded in framing provisions for securing the paying up of capital by subscribing shareholders. The more difficult task was to remove the tendencies towards expansions and to secure note-holders against losses due to suspensions. A major deficiency over the whole of the American banking structure had long been the infrequency of the return of notes to their issuers. One of the earliest and most successful attempts to secure that notes were redeemed more often was a volun-

---

[8] See Gallatin, "Suggestions on the Banks and Currency of the Several United States," p. 36.

[9] See Gallatin, *op. cit.*, p. 49.

tary system put into force by the Suffolk Bank of Massachusetts. Bank-notes circulated at places distant from their issuing bank at discounts varying with the difficulty of sending them home for redemption. The smaller was the chance of its notes being presented for payment, the larger was the volume of notes that a bank could safely issue. The result of the lack of any machinery for ensuring the collection of notes was therefore that banks began purposely to place themselves at long distances from the most important centres of business. This was what happened in Massachusetts. The banks of Boston found themselves at a distinct disadvantage because the country banks were securing practically the entire circulation even in Boston. Large numbers of country bank-notes never returned to the banks that had issued them, but remained in Boston circulating without hindrance at the recognised rate of discount. The Boston banks made several attempts to systemise the sending back of notes for redemption. The most successful was the Suffolk Bank system.[10] This bank arranged for New England country banks to keep with it permanent deposits of $5,000 plus a further sum sufficient to redeem notes reaching Boston. The Suffolk undertook to receive at par the notes of banks who made such deposits, and the notes of country banks who refused to come into the scheme would be sent back for redemption. The Suffolk Bank, moreover, refused admittance to its clearing agency to banks whose integrity was not above suspicion. This had the intended effect of curtailing the circulations of the country banks.

The Massachusetts legislature also passed a law, in 1843, to secure the more frequent return of notes by providing that no bank should pay over its counter any notes but its own. A similar law was passed in Louisiana. Other States placed penalties on the default to pay notes in specie on de-

[10] Started in 1819.

mand, either by the imposition of a percentage tax on the amount involved or by making the offending bank liable to the forfeiture of its charter. This latter measure should have been the most effective if it had been rigidly enforced. Specifications as to reserve requirements also began to emerge in many of the States. The most stringent of these was that of Louisiana requiring a specie reserve of one-third against circulation plus deposits.

In other cases efforts were directed not to preventing the over-issues and ensuring redeemability of notes on demand, but to giving some protection to the note-holder in the actual event of suspensions following such an over-issue. Several States adopted the practice of giving notes a prior lien on assets. Another measure adopted was that of double liability, which made bank shareholders liable for the debts of the bank to an amount equal to their respective holdings of shares over and above the amount of capital actually invested by them in the bank. The most ambitious scheme was the New York Safety-Fund system.[11] This was a system of compulsory insurance of banks against unmet liabilities. The banks paid contributions to a fund to be allocated to the paying out of the liabilities of insolvent banks where they exceeded their assets. There was, of course, a tendency under this scheme to subsidise weak institutions at the expense of the stronger and more prudently managed ones, especially as the insurance premium was not assessed on the basis of actuarial risks, but was merely computed as a percentage on the capital of the bank. It also had the further unhealthy effect of weakening the public scrutiny over the issues of particular banks, and many of the banks were tempted by this fact itself to risk bigger issues. Between 1840 and 1842 eleven of the safety-fund banks failed, the fund was exhausted, and the solvent banks had to be called upon for increased contri-

---

[11] Established in 1829.

butions. Future contributions were also mortgaged in advance for charges in respect of an issue of State bonds made to replenish the fund. After the bankruptcy of the fund in 1842, it was made security for notes only and no longer for deposits as well, but it still proved inadequate.[12]

We have already observed that the banking business in the United States, or at least over the greater part of it, was in the first half century of its growth by no means open to free entry. But from 1838 onwards there was a change of policy in several of the States which made it possible for banks to set up without having to obtain a charter. The new policy was inaugurated by New York in 1838 in a so-called Free-banking Law. Under this law it was made permissible for any person or association to issue notes, provided they had deposited with the Comptroller the equivalent amount in the form of certain securities. All stocks of the United States and those of States approved by the Comptroller were eligible, and, in addition, certain bonds and mortgages on real estate. Should a bank default on its notes, the Comptroller would sell the collateral securities in order to redeem them. The first effect of the newly granted freedom was a wild dash to establish banks.

Immediately on the passage of the bill arrangements were made for the formation of over a hundred and thirty new banks; about half of these had actually started business a year later and nearly half of them had gone out of business after another three years. The idea in the minds of many of the bank organisers seems to have been that if their notes were secured, nobody would ever demand their redemption. Many of them set up solely for the purpose of issuing notes, but in 1848 the State passed legislation requiring banks to undertake discount and deposit business as well as note circulation.

---

[12] The fund was finally wound up in 1866.

The bond deposit system had the effect of tying up bank investment in certain lines, usually Federal or State bonds. Mortgage and other real estate business soon proved to be too illiquid to provide backing for notes. It also had the rather peculiar effect of making the amount of the note circulation depend on the prices of Federal and State bonds. It meant also that while banks, constituted on other lines, could realise their assets in order either to get funds for redeeming their notes or to decrease the amount of notes in circulation, the bond deposit banks had very little chance of doing this, because their capital was tied up in Government securities which they were not free to sell until they had first reduced their note circulation, a feature which put them at a considerable disadvantage in comparison with the chartered banks. Moreover, the system was by no means a perfect guarantee of note redemption, because when a bank failed, many State stocks could be disposed of only at a discount.

Parallel with the beginnings of this movement in favour of a greater measure of competition, there took place in some other States foundations of State monopolies. Early in the nineteenth century Indiana and Illinois had prohibited banks unless the State should judge fit to establish one out of its own funds. The Bank of Indiana and the Bank of Ohio, founded in 1834 and 1845, respectively, were both State monopolies. Illinois followed the New York free banking plan in 1851, and Indiana and Wisconsin did the same a little later.

The improvement that took place in American banking in the twenty years preceding the Civil War was especially noticeable in the eastern region. The banking system was by no means perfect at this period, but except for the international crisis of 1857,[13] when suspensions of specie payments

---

[13] This was yet another occasion when the penalty of liquidation for suspension went to the winds. Under the 1846 Constitution of New York State it was forbidden to the Government to pass any law directly or indirectly sanctioning

were general over most of the United States, the situation was far steadier than ever before. It is very probable that this improvement was not attributable to any considerable extent to State regulations relating to bond deposit guarantees for notes. In fact, the State authorities seem to have become, after a time, rather lax in the enforcement of the law, and the State Comptroller was usually satisfied if the bank had in its own possession the prescribed assets and was prepared to present them for his examination when he paid the bank visits on certain days. This gave scope for a system of window-dressing by which the banks passed round the same block of securities for exhibit on the appropriate days. The law was thereby rendered ineffective. Much the greater weight is to be attached to the more rigid enforcement of specie payments between banks by frequent exchange of notes, due in great part to the spread of the Suffolk system and to the institution of the New York clearing-house.[14]

The Civil War provided the occasion for a radical change in the banking system of the whole country. The banks in the South gave their support to the secession and ceased remittances to the North, and since they had a large net liability towards the banks in the North the latter lost heavily, but they managed to keep above water by contracting their lending operations and were, in fact, in a very strong position regarding specie reserves. Pressure soon came however, from the side of Governmental financial needs. Secretary of the Treasury Chase experienced excessive difficulty in borrowing from the public, partly as a result of the very bad state of the finances in the preceding administration. Chase called a conference of the New York, Boston and Philadelphia banks, and with him they drew up a plan for

suspensions of specie payments, but in the 1857 crisis the authorities refrained from selling out the stocks deposited by the suspending banks and withdrawing their notes; the Courts in New York distinguished between what they called momentary suspensions of specie payments and real insolvency.

[14] 1855.

assisting the Government by advancing $50,000,000. Chase insisted on the loan being paid in specie, and at the same time he started the issue of United States notes payable on demand which further weakened the banks, since if they accepted the Government notes they were obliged to redeem them in coin. The result was that at the turn of the year (1861–62) the banks of New York, Boston and Philadelphia suspended payments. The Treasury followed by ceasing likewise to redeem the Treasury notes in coin. This was followed up by a bill for issuing legal tender irredeemable paper[15] to the extent of $150,000,000, a measure which was strongly opposed by the banks, among others. One of the chief arguments for making the Government notes legal tender was to force the banks to accept them. Two further issues, each of $150,000,000, were made within the twelve months following. After that the issue of greenbacks was stopped, and Chase had recourse to a new scheme for obtaining funds by the sale of Government securities, namely, the National Bank system. This was an extension to a National or Federal, instead of a State, basis of the bond deposit system. By an Act of 1864 banks of not less than five associates, and having a capital of not less than $50,000, were allowed to form freely if they secured their notes by the deposit with the United States Treasurer of registered bonds of the United States. The amount of notes must not be more than 90 percent of the market value of the bonds lodged and not more than 100 percent of their par value. In the event of a bank defaulting on its notes, the United States Treasury would sell the bonds and pay the notes itself. The Treasury also had a prior lien on the general assets of the failed bank for any claims that could not be met out of the proceeds of the bond sales, and, further, the shareholders were subject

---

[15] The notes were lawful money and legal tender in payment of all debts, public and private, within the United States, except for duties on imports and interest on the public debt, which were expressly made payable in coin.

to double liability. The banks must also keep a certain reserve proportion of their notes plus deposits in the form of legal tender currency, which in the years of their foundation meant of course greenbacks as well as specie. The primary motive for setting up this system was, of course, the creation of a large market for Government bonds, but it was contemplated from the beginning that the new National banks would in time replace the old State banks and much emphasis was placed on the benefits of a uniform currency. Provisions were made in the original Act for State banks to come into the scheme by conforming to the conditions of the Act, and, as they failed to come in voluntarily as fast as the Government had hoped, an Act was passed in 1865 to penalise those not entering the system by the imposition of a tax of 10 percent on their note issues. This was practically the death-blow to a great number of the State banks so far as they were dependent on note issue.

In the first years the notes of the National banks were not far short of being legal tender currency, since, although their acceptance between individuals was not compulsory, the Government was to receive them at par in all revenue collections except customs duties and to pay them at par for salaries, wages and debts, except for interest on the public debt and the redemption of greenbacks. Moreover, since lawful money in which notes were to be redeemable meant greenbacks as well as specie, there was an exceptionally large volume of reserve material available against which the National banks could expand their note issues. In spite of all this, by 1867 a large part of the National bank-notes were circulating at a discount against greenbacks and a number of the National banks had already failed in that year.

It seems that people at first placed undue faith in the security of the new notes and perhaps regarded them as not liable to over-issue. For this reason the notes tended to keep out in circulation longer without being sent in to the issuing bank for redemption and there was thus lacking an effective check on the amount that any one bank could keep in circulation, until it was presently realised that it is a mistake to regard a security backing as good as specie.

The really substantial improvement that might have been effected through the National Banking Law was one that the authorities failed to realise, namely, the provision of facilities for a branch banking system. On the contrary, the National banks were forbidden, except under special circumstances, to establish branches.

Some of the peculiarities of the bond deposit system as a means of regulating note issues have already been mentioned in connection with the free banking system of New York. We shall have occasion to refer again to these problems in a later chapter on the American experiences leading up to the Federal Reserve Act.

CHAPTER VI

The Development
of Central Banking
in Germany[1]

The history of banking in Germany, like that of the United States, should properly be considered in terms of the separate States, but it is impossible to do that here and we shall concentrate our attention on the main events in Prussia, with an occasional reference to the policy of other States. The setting in Germany is dissimilar to that in the other countries we have so far considered, for the reason that Germany at no time adopted true *laisser-faire* principles in her commercial policy, and therefore it is less surprising to find State intervention in banking in this country than in any other.

The longer retention of mediaeval restrictions on the free circulation of goods and services witnessed a corresponding lag in the development of banking.[2] But a good deal of literature was written about banks in the early eighteenth century, and there was detectable in most of these writings a mercantilist idea that the setting up of banks would produce a sudden and conspicuous increase in wealth.[3]

---

[1] This chapter is based mainly on the account given by W. Lotz "Geschichte und Kritik des Deutschen Bankgesetzes, vom 14 März, 1875."

[2] In the more modern sense, that is, of discounting and note issue as opposed to the kind of business carried on by the early Giro banks.

[3] *Cf.* H. Schumacher, "Geschichte der deutschen Bankliteratur im 19

The first steps were taken by princes and nobles who, motivated by fiscal needs, attempted to start banking before its time, before commercial conditions were ripe for it, and they consequently met with scant success at least so far as the note-issuing branch of the business was concerned. The first bank of issue to prove at all successful was the Royal Bank of Berlin, a State bank founded by Frederick the Great.[4] It is doubtful whether even this one would have been so fortunate in these years had it not had assigned to it by law certain deposits,[5] and been given also the management of the Exchequer funds. As it began, so it continued, throughout the whole of its existence, as a privileged institution under paternal protection and in close relations with the State. The first effects of this were witnessed in the Napoleonic Wars, when it suspended cash payments with Government sanction. The difficulties of the bank arose in the first place from the heavy loans it made to the Prussian Government, and they were later intensified by losses it suffered as a result of the Peace of Tilsit, which took away from Prussia certain Polish territories in which the bank had invested a large proportion of its deposits on mortgage. These assets were completely lost to the bank. It emerged from the war with an enormous deficit, and after the cessation of hostilities it was reorganised as a result of the war experiences and was made nominally independent of the Treasury and the Finance Minister, but its Chief remained, of course, a State official responsible to the King.

No specific prohibition existed at this time against the formation of private banks other than the obstacles that lay in the way of the establishment of joint stock organisations in all lines of business. In the 'twenties two private banks set up

Jahrhundert" in Schmollers Festschrift, "Die Entwicklung der deutschen Volks-wirtschaftslehre im 19 Jahrhundert," Pt. VII.

[4] In 1765 Frederick was unable to obtain the private capital; otherwise he would have made it a private joint stock bank.

[5] Viz., the moneys of wards, courts and charity institutions.

in Prussia and broke the monopoly of the Royal Bank by undertaking both deposit business and note issue. These were the Berlin Kassenverein and the Pommersche Privatbank at Stettin.[6]

But this period of relative freedom came to an end in 1833, when there was a complete reversal of policy. A law of that year made the issue of all bearer notes dependent on the approval of the Government. This virtual prohibition was prompted not out of regard for the interests of the privileged Royal Bank, it must be noted, but to make way for the circulation of State paper money which had originated in the time of the Napoleonic Wars and was now to be extended. The Royal Bank itself was included in the prohibition; all three of the Prussian note-issuing banks had to give up the issue of notes. These increased restrictions on banking came almost at the very moment when changes in industrial technique were about to swell enormously the demand for credit.

About this time banks were being set up in several other States: the policy in each case was restrictive. In Bavaria the Mortgage and Exchange Bank set up in 1835[7] was given a monopoly of the note issue, not in this case as the result of a desire to give priority to Government notes, of which there were none in Bavaria, but because of the fear that competition in the sphere of note issue would be dangerous, and in accordance with this dread of too many notes, we find a maximum limit to the note issue. A less understandable regulation was that which compelled the bank to invest at least three-fifths of its funds in land loans.

The Leipzig Bank of Saxony, founded in 1838, was not endowed with an exclusive privilege but was subjected to

---

[6] The latter had royal aid at its foundation, and was bolstered up by the Government on several other occasions at a later date.

[7] This was the first note-issuing bank to be set up in Bavaria, but the Royal Bank of Nürnberg, a non-note-issuing bank, dated from 1780.

equally rigid restrictions. In this case the proportional reserve requirement (of two-thirds) was imposed in preference to the maximum limit on the note issue.

It was in the 'forties that the struggle for free trade in banking became acute. In the preceding years capital had been relatively abundant and interest rates low, but about the middle of the decade a reversion set in as the result of increased capital needs for railway development, and interest rates rose. The public mind entertained exaggerated hopes as to the power of banking. It was a widespread belief that all that was necessary to relieve a scarcity of capital was an elastic note issue, and the issue of notes was still thought to possess something akin to a magic power of transforming poverty into wealth. The philosophy of the Saint Simonians, which conceived of a reformed society in which the banking system was given a central organising role in the assembly and distribution of capital, had also spread to Germany. These notions gave an impetus to two movements, the one demanding increased note issues and the other looking towards the creation of *crédit mobilier* institutions.

Added to the demand for more capital, there was at this time a genuine currency difficulty. Very little gold was then in circulation, and in the absence of notes, payments had to be made in silver, which was very heavy to carry out. Notes were therefore found of very great convenience, and since they were relatively scarce, they were often sought even at a premium. There began an agitation against the repression of private initiative, and the Prussian Government was overwhelmed with schemes for the creation of private banks of issue to exist alongside the Royal Bank, all of which it strongly opposed. The demand for private initiative took two forms. One group merely wanted a private joint stock bank in place of the existing State bank; others wanted to go much further and demanded nothing less than a system of independent freely-organised competitive banks.

The Prussian Government was led out of passivity into action by the news that on one of its borders in the neighbouring state of Dessau the authorities had approved the project for a note-issuing bank which had plans for extending its activities over the border into Prussia. Although William IV commissioned Rother, the then Minister at the head of the Royal Bank, to work out a scheme for the establishment of private banks of issue, Rother dismissed the idea as being of not more than mere academic interest, and adopted the much less liberal alternative of reorganising the Royal Bank. This bank was still handicapped by lack of capital arising from the deficit left by the French Wars, and the scheme that was adopted was intended to replenish the assets of the bank and so strengthen its lending capacity. Rother certainly envisaged a State bank as the most desirable, but, probably owing to the lack of funds in the State Treasury, he fell back on the introduction of private share capital into the bank. So it was reconstituted in 1846 as the Prussian Bank, now partly controlled by private shareholders instead of wholly by the State. It was given back the right of note issue which it had formerly exercised, and its notes were gradually to replace the State paper then in circulation, but the law specified *both* a maximum limit to the note issue *and* a metal reserve proportion to the extent of one-third[8] of the note circulation. The bank retained the privileges it had held as the Royal Bank, and its notes were made legal tender for public transactions. An important clause in the decree establishing the bank and characteristic of the banking notions of

[8] The "Dritteldeckung" (cash reserve of one-third), which from this time onwards was a common provision in the laws on German banks of issue, seems to have been the adoption by legal prescription of the conventional practice said by Horsley Palmer to have been followed by the Bank of England before the Commission of 1832 in England. Palmer's pamphlet on the policy of the Bank of England prior to the crisis of 1836–7, which we mentioned in a previous chapter, was translated into German under the title "Die Ursachen und Folgen der Wirksamkeit der Bank von England in dem Zeitraume vom 10 Oktober 1833 bis 27 Dezember, 1836" (1837).

the period was that which stated specifically that it was its express task to prevent any great rise in the rate of interest, and it was, in fact, forbidden to raise the rate for lombard business above 6 percent.

But the extension of the note issue and the lending powers of the Prussian Bank did not suffice to quieten the agitation for greater freedom. The year 1847 was a year of very heavy demand for credit. This was especially true of the west, in the lower Rhineland and Westphalia, where industrial development was proceeding fast, and, although provision had been made in the constitution of the Prussian Bank for the establishment of branches, it had been particularly slow to develop them in these parts. Opinion in favour of private note-issuing banks became very strong, and its adherents began to hold organised discussions on the subject.[9]

The excitement of 1848 brought a sharp turn of events. The Government was persuaded to allow note-issuing powers to the Bank of Breslau and to the Chemnitzer Stadtbank; it also set up itself State loan banks in connection with the Prussian Bank; finally, it took the far more radical step of granting concessions for the creation of private note-issuing banks. But this was only a very grudging gift to the free-banking party; the concession was in each case given for a period of ten years only, and, moreover, the banks were over-regulated in the extreme. The celebrated *Normativ-Bedingungen*, under which they were established, restricted the scope of their business to a minimum. Besides the stipulation that they must keep a metal reserve of one-third against their note issue, they were tied down to the smallest possible level of funds, and the lines of business in which they might engage were likewise restricted. Their paid-up capital must not exceed a certain very low figure. The maxi-

---

[9] As in the *Erste Vereinigte Landtag* in 1847.

mum note issue for all the provinces together was fixed at a figure only one-third of the limit for the Prussian Bank and this total was divided equally among the provinces with no regard to their relative business needs. The banks were not allowed to have agents in other centres; they were not allowed to deal in Government securities that were not Prussian; neither could they discount bills whose acceptor lived outside the business place of the bank, and bills must be three-named; moreover, they were not allowed to pay interest on deposits, thus leaving such business entirely in the hands of the Prussian Bank. So urgent was the demand for notes, however, that the Berliner Kassenverein and the Stettin Bank[10] immediately subjected themselves to these regulations in order to be able to exercise rights of issue.

Alongside the note issue campaign a second notion was beginning to exert an influence on the development of banking institutions in Germany. Almost as soon as the *crédit mobilier* idea was first evolved in France it was taken up in Germany, and by the turn of the decade a number of joint stock banks were setting up in various parts of Germany in *crédit mobilier* business. The Disconto-Gessellschaft in Berlin, the Schaffhausen'schen Bankverein in Cologne and the Darmstadter were among the most important. In Prussia it was still difficult to establish even these, since joint stock companies had to obtain special Government concession before they were allowed to go into business. So it was that the Bank für Handel und Industrie (later known as the Darmstadter) had to set up at Darmstadt because no concession could be obtained at the time either in Prussia or in Frankfurt am Main, and the Disconto-Gesellschaft was a partnership for six years before it could obtain a concession to become a joint stock concern.

The rate of progress in the setting up of note-issuing banks

---

[10] The Stettin Bank was allowed to retain its interest-bearing deposits.

was slow,[11] and did not go far to meet the demands of the Free Banking Party. Under the leadership of Harkort in the Chamber of Deputies, this party secured the institution in 1851–2 of a parliamentary enquiry into banking and credit conditions in Prussia, and via these channels it gained more public attention. On the positive side the party demanded a relaxation of the *Normativ-Bedingungen,* and on the negative side it declaimed against the Prussian Bank as a half-State institution standing in the way of private enterprise. Harkort tried hard but unsuccessfully to get legislation passed for the removal of the *Normativ-Bedingungen.*

Some reforms did take place in the policy of the Prussian Bank; it began to adopt a more liberal lending policy[12] and also extended its branches in the western provinces.

In the smaller States note-issuing banks were being founded in considerable numbers, and their notes soon began to circulate just over the boundary in Prussia and Saxony. These small States issued notes for lower denominations than the Prussian Bank, and the Prussian Government sought to exclude them from its territory by forbidding payments in non-Prussian notes for sums less than 10 Rthlr. Saxony, Bavaria and Württemberg followed the same course, but the laws had no effect because the banks against whom they were aimed merely replaced their 1 Rthlr. notes by 10 Rthlr. notes.

The Prussian Government saw that the only logical solution was to increase the note issue inside Prussia. Two

[11] The total result of all the concessions even up to 1857 was that in that year there were in Prussia nine note-issuing banks, including the Bank of Prussia.

[12] It started the practice of lending out part of its deposits on current account. Much of the progress in Prussia during these years had been due to the efforts of one man, David Hansemann. It was under his leadership as President of the Bank that the Prussian Bank changed its policy. He had also been responsible as Finance Minister for obtaining the 1848 concessions for the formation of private note-issuing banks and for securing the royal consent to the foundation of the Schaffenhausen'schen Bankverein as a joint stock company. It was again he who, a few years later, founded the Disconto-Gesellschaft.

alternative ways of doing this were conceivable. One was to change the law relating to the foundation of private banks and the other to centralise the banking system, and give unlimited rights of note issue to the Prussian Bank. Finally a compromise was adopted. The Government gave unlimited rights of note issue to the Prussian Bank and allowed it to issue notes of low denominations in return for a financial operation which the Government regarded as very favourable to itself, namely, the commutation of half of its State paper money into interest-bearing State debt. Secondly, concessions were made in favour of private note-issuing banks. Four more received Government sanction to set up, and certain of the clauses of the *Normativ-Bedingungen* were modified so as to allow the private banks to discount two-named bills, to set up agencies, to issue small notes, and to take interest-bearing deposits. The concession regarding interest-bearing deposits was subject to the condition that the amount taken must not exceed the amount of the original capital of the bank, and that the deposits should not be callable at less than two months' notice.

Then the crisis of 1857 occurred, and this had a marked effect on the later trend of policy. It provoked a reaction against the bank creations of the 'fifties[13] and brought the beginnings of a change in attitude. The Prussian Bank was accused of having kept the discount rate too low before the crisis, and one good effect that came of it was the renunciation of the limitation of the rate of interest to 6 percent. In the crisis itself the bank assumed what had come to be considered the functions of a central bank by lending freely to reputable firms who found themselves in difficulties. The unlimited right of issue of the Prussian Bank was denounced, and there was a crop of literature in favour of a

---

[13] Although there were still in 1858 only thirty *Zettelbanken* in twenty States.

100 percent specie backing for the note issue.[14] The small *Zettelbanken* of the border States were condemned, probably justifiably in many cases, since they had attempted the impossible thing of combining *crédit mobilier* business with note issue. Steps were taken to exclude their notes both in Prussia and in Saxony. The Prussian Government forbade all payments in non-Prussian bank-notes. In Saxony the prohibition of foreign notes was to apply only if the note-issuing bank had no redemption centre in Saxony. The law was in either case ineffective in preventing the circulation of foreign notes; all that happened was that the notes went to a discount because of the risk of legal punishment.

The Prussian Chamber of Deputies was by now divided into many factions over the banking question, ranging from a leaning towards full freedom for all banks to issue notes at the one extreme to a preference for complete unity in the note issue at the other. The latter was as yet unpractical because of the impossibility of keeping out the notes of the border States, and Prussia's negotiations to obtain uniformity of policy among the separate States met with little success. The systematic discussion of the whole banking question together with the formulation of a positive programme was taken up by a private association of free traders, the *Kongress deutscher Volkswirte*, foremost among whom was Dr. Otto Michaelis. The free-banking (*Bankfreiheit*) party had already somewhat changed its ground. *Bankfreiheit* without any State intervention was no longer so prominent and was beginning to be relegated to a position of purely academic interest. The Congress opposed the too lax regulations of the *"wilden Banken"* of the border States, but condemned the over-supervision of the *Normativ-Bedingungen*. They had by this time given up all hope of ever securing freedom for private banks in note issue, and henceforth concentrated their

[14] Notable exponents of this view were Tellkampf and Geyer. See Chapter IX.

efforts on trying to secure freedom for deposit banking, on a joint stock basis, pointing out that it was unfortunate that people persisted in regarding note issue as the chief object of banking.

The swing towards increasing freedom in the note issue was slowing up. It received practically its last acknowledgment in 1863 when certain of the restrictions on private note-issuing banks were slightly modified; they were allowed to take additional interest-bearing deposits, the limit now being twice instead of once the amount of their paid-up capital, and the period of their concession was extended from ten to fifteen years. In the Chamber of Deputies there was still a good deal of criticism of the Prussian Bank, and most especially of its unlimited right of note issue, and Michaelis was recommending the passing of a Peel's Act for Germany.

In the south of Germany the restrictions were still very stringent. Where there was not monopoly there was complete prohibition of note issue, as was the case in Baden and Württemberg. In both these States the Governments had persistently opposed the establishment of a note-issuing bank, and it was only in the Franco-Prussian War that one was conceded for the first time.

Most forces were now operating in the direction of securing further centralisation. The 1866 crisis impressed many observers with the advantages of a strong bank which can give liberal accommodation in a crisis. The continual consolidation of political authorities helped to widen the area over which a common policy could be pursued. Prussia acquired new territories after the war of 1866 to which the business of the Prussian Bank was extended, and the *Norddeutscher Bund* in 1870 gained control over banking legislation in all the member States. A reform of the law relating to joint stock companies freed them from the obligation to obtain authoritative concession, and this at last opened the way to the establishment of non-note-issuing banks, which was all that the free-banking party now demanded. The final impulse to the adoption of central banking was given to Germany's experiences in the first years of her operation of the gold standard.

At the formation of the Reich in 1871 the laws of the *Norddeutscher Bund* were extended to the whole of German territory and a uniform currency was established for the first time; it was based on the gold standard, and the payment of the French indemnity provided an easy opportunity for accumulating the necessary reserves.

As early as 1873 a crisis occurred, however. The note issues of those banks which had had no maximum limit or which had never previously reached their limit had risen very rapidly after 1871, and this was especially true of the Prussian Bank. When the French indemnity stopped, the exchanges went against Germany, and gold started to flow out. Germany had had very little experience of external specie flows, because when silver had been the standard it had been very expensive to collect specie and export it, and the specie points had therefore been very wide. Neither were the Germans familiar with the effect of a gold flow in rectifying the exchanges, and the immediate consequences of the first gold exports was a scare that all the gold was going out and that Germany would be off the gold standard. The undue alarm that thus arose had an important influence on bank policy. It brought in the first place a sudden realisation of the uses of discount policy. German opinion had been very much influenced by English events, and especially by Peel's Act, and following on English doctrine, it was believed that in order to manipulate a discount policy it was necessary to have a specially constituted central bank, which would be responsible for controlling specie flows.

These ideas were embodied in the German Bank of 1875.[15] The Act was closely modelled on the English Act of 1844, but

---

[15] Both Tellkampf and Michaelis took part in the drafting.

far more statutory requirements were imposed. The position of the private note banks was as follows: Thirty-three note-issuing banks were recognised for the whole of the Reich and no new ones might be established. The fiduciary issues of all the banks, including the Reichsbank, were given a legal maximum, and a reserve proportion of one-third against their total note issue was also imposed. If any bank relinquished its issue, the Reichsbank was to acquire an addition to the same amount to its legal fiduciary issue. Submission to the terms of the Act involved disabilities, however, in the form of a restriction on certain types of business. Thus, if banks wanted to continue to issue notes they must not engage in acceptance business; they might trade only in certain classes of bonds, must not engage in mortgage business, and could not discount bills having more than three months to run.

The Reichsbank was constituted out of the old Prussian Bank, which was turned into a wholly privately owned concern, but retained the official administration with still very little control left in the hands of the shareholders; it was consequently considerably less independent of Government control than the Bank of England. The business of the Reichsbank was restricted to certain lines: discount and lombard business was subject to the same limitations as in the case of the private banks, and the taking of interest-bearing deposits was permissible only up to a fixed sum. The notes of the Reichsbank were not made legal tender, but they were given much wider circulation than the notes of private banks, in that, whereas a private bank might not pay out notes of any other private bank except to the issuing bank or for payment to the place wherein the issuing bank was situated, notes of the Reichsbank might be paid out by the receiving bank without restriction.

A private note-issuing bank was allowed to stay out from the provisions of the Act, but if it did this it was to have its operations restricted to the territory of the State which gave it its right of note issue.

The provisions of this Act secured to the Reichsbank the position of a modern central bank.

CHAPTER VII

Discussions on the Theory of the Subject in England and America Prior to 1848

Although the discussion of free banking had its beginning in England, it never reached such large proportions there as it did on the Continent. This may have been due to the much greater degree of freedom that had always existed in England giving rise to a more rapid growth of banking there than in either France or Germany, and therefore to a less pressing need for reform. Moreover, by the time *laisser-faire* politics had taken up its stand against privileged monopolies, the Bank of England and the system of which it had become the pivot were far too well established to be easily remodelled, whereas on the Continent the banking systems were less firmly established and therefore more subject to discussion.

The discussion in England seems to have opened in connection with the agitation for joint stock banking, commencing with the pamphlet of Thomas Joplin,[1] of 1822, in which attention was drawn to the greater stability and freedom

[1] "The General Principles and Present Practice of Banking in England and Scotland: with Observations on the Justice and Policy of an Immediate Alteration in the Character of the Bank of England, and the Measures to be pursued in order to effect it."

from failures of the Scottish banks in comparison with the English, a circumstance which he attributed to the greater financial strength and general superiority of the joint stock organisation in which the number of subscribing sharehold-ers was unrestricted compared with private concerns in which the number of the partners was by law not allowed to rise above six. It was impossible to ignore the anomalies of a law which, as Lord Liverpool remarked, permitted "every description of banking except that which is solid and secure."[2]

The partial victory of what we may already call the free-banking party, in the law of 1826, gave added impetus to the general discussion, and it was brought forward at several meetings of the Political Economy Club. This club had been founded by Tooke to support the principles of Free Trade, and it was not unnatural that reference should be made to the possibilities of extending Free Trade principles to bank-ing. The chief adherent of such an extension was Sir Henry Parnell, who moved a discussion[3] on whether "a proper cur-rency (might not) be secured by leaving the business of banking wholly free from all legislative interference." Much the same question was brought up on several subsequent occasions.[4] Parnell continued to hold that the issue of bank notes should be subject to free entry in London as well as in the provinces, and not subject to the monopoly of the Bank of England, although three of the leading economists of the day, Tooke, G. W. Norman and MacCulloch, argued against him.

Parnell's defence of free banking is contained in a pam-

---

[2] See J. Horsley Palmer, "Causes and Consequences of the Pressure on the Money Market," 1837.
[3] See "Political Economy Club: Minutes of Proceedings," Vol.VI., February 6th, 1826 (p. 28).
[4] *Ibid.*, May 4th, 1829 (p. 33); January 13th, 1831 (pp. 220–1); March 1st, 1832 (p. 38 and pp. 231–2); May 3rd, 1832 (p. 39).

phlet written in 1827.[5] The evidence of the Scotch bankers before the House of Commons Committee[6] in 1826 had drawn his attention to the practice of the Scotch banks in regularly clearing each other's notes and paying the balances. This practice, he submitted, was of primary importance in a free-banking system and acted as a very efficient check on the over-issue of bank notes. He contended that in a free system it was in the interests of each bank not only to keep its own issues within bounds, but also to exert its power in preventing every other bank from forcing too much of its paper into circulation.[7] Banks will receive every day from customers, either as deposits or in repayment of loans, notes of other banks, and no banks will re-issue the notes of other banks in preference to issuing its own. It will return the notes of the other banks to their issuers. Now if any bank A receives by such means more notes of bank B than B receives of A's notes, there will arise a clearing balance in favour of A, and A will require to be paid in gold out of B's reserve. So it is concluded that if one bank over-issued its notes the other banks would acquire positive balances against it, and the consequent drain on its reserve would pull it up in its expansion. This control by way of the clearing mechanism was one which depended not on the *public's* presenting notes for redemption but on the *banks'* reciprocally doing so, and it was a check which was likely to work much more quickly than one which waited on the external drain of bullion set in motion by the falling foreign exchange rates. In Parnell's own words: "It is this continual demand for coin, by the banks on one another, that gives the principle of convertibility full effect, and no such thing as an excess of paper or as a depreciation of its value can take place

[5] "Observations on Paper Money, Banking and Overtrading, including those parts of the evidence taken before the Committee of the House of Commons which explained the Scotch System of Banking."

[6] Committee of the House of Commons on Scotch Banking.

[7] *Op. cit.*, pp. 86–87.

for want of a sufficiently early and active demand for gold. If in England the power of converting paper into gold has not prevented an excess of paper, because the demand does not occur until long after the excess has taken place, this is to be attributed to the system of English banking."[8]

The opposition between the views of Parnell and MacCulloch was given more definite expression in a pamphlet of MacCulloch's[9] and a reply to that pamphlet by Parnell.[10] MacCulloch's contribution contains the first important theoretical arguments for the case against free banking. So far as the whole circulation of the country is concerned, his view was that so long as convertibility on demand is enforced, the issue of paper money cannot depreciate its value below that of coin. An over-issue can admittedly depress the value of the whole circulation, gold as well as paper, in the country concerned, but immediately this over-issue takes place, gold starts going abroad, notes are presented to the issuers for payment, and they, in order to prevent the exhaustion of their reserves and to maintain their ability to redeem their obligations, are obliged to contract their issues, raise the value of money and stop the gold efflux. There is, therefore, in his opinion always a check on over-issues by way of the public's bringing notes to the banks for redemption. Now on the evidence of this argument alone it was open for Parnell to reply, as in fact he did, that the obligations to pay notes in gold, which MacCulloch invoked as a safeguard against the Bank's over-issuing its notes, is just as effective in a system of a number of banks as in the case of a single bank like the Bank of England, that, in fact, this Bank had often over-

[8] *Op. cit.,* p. 88.
[9] "Historical Sketch of the Bank of England with an Examination of the Question as to the prolongation of the exclusive privileges of that Establishment," 1831.
[10] "A Plain Statement of the Power of the Bank of England and the Use it has made of it; with a Refutation of the Objections made to the Scotch System of Banking, and a Reply to the Historical Sketch of the Bank of England," 1832.

issued and that the principle of contraction had worked very imperfectly in these cases because the Bank had always applied it too late.

MacCulloch had, however, developed his argument further than this in an attempt to show that the free system of banking would be more liable than a restricted system to lead to the frequent appearance of the phenomena of over-issue, the reason being that competition among a number of banks would cause one bank to lower its discount rate in order to increase its business, and all banks would be forced to do the same. He anticipates that his opponents might argue that the notes of the bank, taking the initiative in the process of expansion, would be returned to it and that, therefore, its own interest and the integrity of its reserves would hold it back. In reply to this argument he denies that any such check would operate because when falling exchange rates cause merchants to demand gold in exchange for notes they will send in for redemption any notes that first come into their hands. They will not enquire which bank has been the cause of the over-issue, and consequently only the same proportion[11] of the excess issue will be returned to the over-issuing bank as to the non-over-issuing banks. Thus the non-over-issuing banks have to sustain part of the pressure, and if they wanted to maintain their reserves at the same level as before they would have to reduce their issues while the policy of the expanding bank continued to encroach on their reserves. It is exceedingly unlikely that these banks would be content to go on losing business and reserves indefinitely, because carried to extremes the process would finally result in their extinction and in the *de facto* monopoly of the expanding bank. They would thus be virtually forced to follow the policy of expansion in self-de-

---

[11] It would be more practical to assume that the proportions in which notes are returned to each bank are the same as the proportions existing between the circulations outstanding of the different banks.

fence. The conclusion is that if one bank should decide on such a policy, it will become general; the tendency to a drain of gold will fail to check it in its early stages; there will be a large over-issue and finally a very acute crisis.

The essence of MacCulloch's thesis is that the expanding bank is not subservient to the control of the conservative banks, but that the latter are, on the contrary, subservient to the former. It should be noted that MacCulloch spoke only of the presentation of notes for gold directly by the public, a check that can be held in any case to come too late, since the exchanges are only affected after the over-issue has worked out its effects on the price and production structure and sown the seeds of a crisis. He ignored altogether Parnell's point about the operation of the clearing mechanism.

MacCulloch gives also a second and distinct reason for not allowing free entry into the note-issuing business. This relates not so much to the possibilities of a general over-issue, but to the evils that may result from over-issue on the part of a single bank or a number of banks. It is obvious that when a failure of any particular bank occurs, certain people, viz., the holders of the notes of that bank, will suffer loss, and it was MacCulloch's view that the Government should regulate banking in order to prevent such loss accruing to people who were possibly unable to distinguish the note of a good house from the note of a bad house, or, even if they did have sufficient knowledge to do this, might in practice not be in a position to refuse to accept payment in the notes of any form for fear of losing their claims altogether.[12] This is a particularly forceful argument in favour of the suppression of notes

[12] *Op. cit.*, pp. 8–9. "It is said by those who are hostile to interference that coins are legal tenders whereas notes being destitute of that privilege, those who suspect them are at liberty to refuse them; but whatever notes may be in law, they are in many districts practically and in fact legal tenders, and could not be rejected without exposing the parties to much inconvenience. It should also be observed, that labourers, women, minors and every sort of person, however incapable of judging the stability of banking establishments, are dealers in money and are consequently liable to be imposed upon."

of small denomination, since it is the class of people who will not usually be in receipt at any one time of sums above a fairly small amount (say less than £5) who are mainly concerned. Actually the argument that MacCulloch himself stresses in favour of the prohibition of £1 notes is the greater facility with which forged notes of small denomination are likely to pass.[13]

Another argument, in support of which MacCulloch gives very little evidence, is that whereas the Bank of England takes care to keep gold reserves of a size commensurable with demands liable to arise in time of a crisis, if there were a number of competitive banks, no particular bank would incur any sort of general public responsibility and each would trust to the efforts of the others. This was, as stated, an argument that was weak *a priori,* and for which there was, furthermore, little practical evidence.

Influenced no doubt by the experiences of 1825 he was led also to remark on the advantages of an institution like the Bank of England, which could render aid during a crisis by expanding its issues and lending freely to reputable firms in distress. With the alternative system of a number of firms, no bank would be able to inspire the same confidence and to get its notes accepted; in time of general distrust they would all have to contract their operations instead of expanding them.

Parnell's reply to MacCulloch was directed mainly towards a criticism of the policy in the previous half century of the Bank of England, and no attempt was made to answer MacCulloch's main grounds of objection to a diffusion of the rights of note issue.

Events in America at about this time were also calling forth comments from writers in that country on the problems raised by the issue of bank-notes. An influential

[13] Presumably notes for smaller sums are likely to be subjected to less careful scrutiny than notes involving larger sums.

contribution was made by Albert Gallatin at the beginning of the 'thirties.[14] In reviewing American banking history he was inevitably most impressed by the frequency of suspensions of cash payments and was chiefly interested to discover effective methods of controlling note issues within their proper limits. To this end he recommended the placing of much narrower limitations, both on the amount of the note issue and on other obligations that any bank might legally incur.[15] He believed that the best method of giving complete security against the danger of insolvency was for the bank capital to be invested in Government securities,[16] but he doubted whether this would be practicable in the United States because there was not a large volume of Government stocks in existence. He was, however, very favourably impressed by the Scottish system,[17] and refers to the extensive deposit business and the system of cash credits[18] developed by the Scottish banks. The most efficacious method of preventing excessive issues was, he believed, the frequent exchange of each other's notes by the banks as practised successfully by the Scottish banks, the allied banks of Boston and the Bank of the United States.[19]

In spite of his praise of the Scottish system, Gallatin was not in favour of extending free competition to note issue as opposed to discount and deposit business. He did not explain the distinction by reasoning as did so many of his contemporaries that deposits, unlike bank-notes, had no effect

[14] "Considerations on the Currency and Banking System of the United States," 1831.

[15] The figure he suggested was that loans should not extend beyond twice the amount of bank capital. This would in itself act as a check on issues, but he recommended that in addition there should be a specific restriction of the note issue to two-thirds of the bank's capital.

[16] The bond deposit system proved, in fact, later, that it was far from adequate.

[17] Op. cit., p. 94.

[18] This corresponded more or less to what we should now call the method of loan by overdraft.

[19] Op. cit., p. 95.

on the total circulation and therefore on prices. On the contrary, he specifically states that "The credits in current account or deposits of our banks are also in their origin and effect perfectly assimilated to bank-notes—and we cannot therefore but consider the aggregate amount of credits payable on demand standing on the books of the several banks as being part of the currency of the United States."[20] There is no doubt that he saw clearly not only the part played by checks drawn on current account on the total amount of circulating media, but also the exact similarity between creating additional loans by placing credits to current account as by issuing notes over the counter. Presumably the reason he had in mind for distinguishing between notes and deposits was the difference in generality of acceptability.[21]

Among Gallatin's readers was G. W. Norman, a Director of the Bank of England.[22] Norman rejected the thesis of Gallatin and Parnell that the clearing mechanism can act as an efficient control over note issues; he reasons that if the will to expand is common to all or to a majority of the banks the frequent exchange of notes will be powerless as a check on over-issues, because so long as the banks expand in step with one another, no debits will arise in the clearings.

It was his own view that while what he calls "the true and legitimate objects of banking" could and ought to be left to free competition,[23] note issue was the one case in a hundred where monopoly should be maintained,[24] and he favoured to this end the complete abolition of all the country note issues.[25]

---

[20] *Op. cit.*, p. 31.

[21] "Checks differ from bank issues in that the bank-note is taken in payment solely from the general confidence reposed in the banks, the check from the special confidence placed in the drawer." See Gallatin, "Suggestions on the Banks and Currency of the Several United States, etc.," 1841, p. 13.

[22] "Remarks on Currency and Banking," 1833.

[23] *Op. cit.*, pp. 27 and 42.

[24] *Op. cit.*, pp. 25–26.

[25] *Op. cit.*, p. 58.

The first writer to give an explicit explanation of why competition in note issue cannot be assimilated to competition in other trades seems to be have been S. J. Loyd (later Lord Overstone). "The ordinary advantages to the community arising from competition are," he says, "that it tends to excite the ingenuity and exertion of the producers, and thus to secure to the public the best supply, due regard being had to the quality and quantity of the commodity, at the lowest price, while all the evils arising from errors or miscalculations on the part of the producers will fall on themselves and not on the public. With respect to a paper currency, however, the interest of the public is of a very different kind; a steady and equable regulation of its amount by fixed law is the end to be sought and the evil consequence of any error or miscalculation upon this point falls in a much greater proportion upon the public than upon the issuers."[26]

Loyd, Norman and MacCulloch were all in later years to become prominent members of the currency school and adherents of Peel's Act. It is therefore less surprising to find them among the opponents of free entry into the banking trade than it is to find Tooke in the same camp, for he, besides being one of the leaders of the Free Trade movement, was the foremost representative of that school of thought on currency and credit which came to be known as the banking school. This group was opposed to the imposition of legal restrictions on the amount of the note issue, and thought it should be left to the discretion of the note-issuing authorities under the force of the demand of the public, to determine the amount. In spite of the support he gave to these views[27] Tooke was violently opposed to leaving banking open to free trade. "As to free trade in banking in the sense in which it is sometimes contended for," he said, "I agree

---

[26] From his pamphlet entitled "Further Reflections on the State of the Currency and the Action of the Bank of England," 1837, p. 49.

[27] At least by 1840.

with a writer in one of the American papers, who observes
that free trade in banking is synonymous with free trade in
swindling." Such claims "do not rest in any manner on
grounds analogous to the claims of freedom of competition
in production—. It is a matter for regulation by the State and
comes within the province of police."[28] This dictum of
Tooke's was quoted times out of number by opponents of
free banking on the Continent and became for them something in the nature of a motto.

The 1837 cash suspensions in America again led to
renewed discussion on that side of the Atlantic, and these
discussions exercised considerable influence on later Continental thought. Two writers, Richard Hildreth and H. C.
Carey, made out a strong case for free banking. Hildreth[29]
denounced the protectionist spirit prevailing in American
banking and contended that if free competition were allowed to replace the existing system of political interference
and monopoly, there would be far fewer excesses. Carey[30]
defended the American banking system on the whole, pointing out that even if not satisfactory in all respects it provided
more facilities than the banks of any other country, and he
maintained that failures had in fact been less frequent than
in England.[31] In a comparative study of the various systems
applied by different States within America he found that
where entry into the banking trade was most free, failures
were least frequent, and he submitted that the whole principle behind the restrictive system was bound to lead to over-
expansions, for, he says, "the system of privilege in banking
arises from the erroneous idea that banking is different from

---

[28] "History of Prices," 1838, Vol. III., p. 206.
[29] "The History of Banks to which is added a Demonstration of the Advantages and Necessity of Free Competition in the Business of Banking," 1837.
[30] "The Credit System in France, Great Britain, and the United States," 1838.
[31] He says that from the first institution of banks in America until 1837 the
failures had been less than those of England in the three years 1814, 1815 and
1816.

all other trades; that it affords the means of making large profits, and that the right to bank should be held as a privilege to be sold to a few individuals. Communities acting under this false impression demand large bonuses for its use, *thus imposing upon the parties a necessity for trading much beyond their capital.*"[32] The Scotch system, although superior to the English, he regarded as still not entirely satisfactory, because it did not allow banks to form with limited liability.[33]

The weakest part of Carey's work was the theoretical explanation he invoked in support of the thesis that a restricted banking system is more likely to cause economic crises.[34] The argument he gives is one that gained some considerable following later in France and which is generally, though erroneously, believed to have been started by Coquelin. It begins by assuming that if there are only one or a few privileged banks, there will be a scarcity of long-term investments. Part of those available will have been bought by the banks themselves and the public will possess in the form of savings a quantity of spare funds for which at the moment there is no very profitable outlet in investment. These funds will consequently be left on deposit at the banks. On the basis of this the banks will be in a position to extend their issues, and they will, in doing so, make liquid capital still further superabundant and deposits will again increase. The process will repeat itself until at last the depositors find an outlet for their funds, let us say abroad, and therefore withdraw their deposits from the banks, thus causing an embarrassment to the latter, who are forced to call in their loans, and a scarcity of capital ensues. All this arises because as a result of the first impediment to investments a great deal of capital has been only temporarily lent

[32] *Op. cit.,* p. 89. Italics ours.
[33] *Op. cit.,* pp. 80–82.
[34] *Op. cit.,* pp. 57 ff.

to the banks but has been invested by them in forms that cannot be immediately liquidated.[35] The theory contends that if more banks were allowed to set up, the bank stocks themselves would provide the public with opportunities for direct investment, and instead of these funds being lent to the banks only on short term they would be lent on long term and there would be less tendency to disturbance.[36]

In contrast a very unfavourable attitude towards American banking was taken up by Condy Raguet.[37] His book was of a more general and theoretical nature than Carey's and tried to sketch the whole of the theory of money and credit relevant to the suspensions of specie payments. He pointed out that the principle of the balance of trade and specie flow adjustments which was already familiar in the theory of international exchange was equally applicable to the balance of claims arising out of the issues of different banks in the same town or groups of banks in different towns, and if allowed to function, this principle would keep the issues of individual banks in check. This emphasised the importance of enforcing immediate redemption of notes on demand, and of the frequent exchange of notes and payment of balances between banks. Unlike Carey, he thought the best system would be to establish individual responsibility (unlimited liability) of the shareholders, but doubted whether such a system could ever be put into practice in the United States where the limited liability form of company organisation was far too deeply rooted. He was strongly opposed to freedom to issue notes in the wide sense but was very favourably disposed towards the New York bond deposit system. His explanation of how an over-supply of credit leads first to an industrial boom and then to a crisis contains

---

[35] P. 57 n.: "The loans of banks to individuals are temporary, but as regards the community at large they may be deemed permanent."

[36] P. 59.

[37] "Treatise on Money and Banking," 1839.

points which anticipate modern trade cycle theory. The end of the boom comes when there is a demand for coin for exportation; the banks are called upon to pay their notes and must in turn call upon their debtors; so money becomes scarce and the prices of property and commodities fall. "At the winding up of the catastrophe, it is discovered that during the whole of this operation *consumption* has been increasing faster than *production*—that the community is poorer in the end than when it began—that instead of food and clothing it has railroads and canals adequate for the transportation of double the quantity of produce and merchandise that there is to be transported—and that the whole of the appearance of prosperity which was exhibited while the currency was gradually increasing in quantity was like the appearance of wealth and affluence which the spendthrift exhibits while running through his estate, and like it, destined to be followed by a period of distress and inactivity."[38]

A fourth contribution was another essay by Gallatin.[39] This is in the main a plea for the rapid resumption of specie payments. He had by this time adopted an attitude that was unfavourable to paper issues in general. He consequently takes up the point of view that there should be a shift of emphasis away from the issue of notes to other banking facilities such as exchange operations, the remittance of money, the collection of debts, the investment of idle balances, all of which could be carried on without the issue of paper money, and he looks forward to the time when banks will set up for these purposes without possessing rights of note issue. He distinguished two senses of the term "free banking"[40]— "First, that all persons or associations should be permitted to

[38] *Op. cit.,* p. 137. Italics in the original.
[39] "Suggestions on the Banks and Currency of the Several United States in Reference principally to the Suspension of Specie Payments," 1841.
[40] *Op. cit.,* p. 69.

issue paper money on the same terms; secondly, that paper money may be issued by all persons or associations, without any legislative restrictions." The first sense in which, after the New York legislation of 1838, the term came almost exclusively to be used by English-speaking writers, Gallatin was prepared to uphold, but competition in general was not applicable to banking[41] because the objects that it attained in the case of the production of a commodity, viz., a reduction in the cost or an improvement in the quality were not relevant to banking.

We have referred already on several occasions to the contention of the free-banking school that there exists in the competitive system an automatic mechanism which operates to check expansions of the note issue. The mechanism consists in the return of notes for gold to the bank or banks that over-issue. It has been already rejected (by MacCulloch) in so far as it depends on the presentation of notes by the public for gold. But it was held also to work through the reciprocal claims of the banks themselves upon each other's reserves. We have mentioned, too, the objection (of Norman) that this also would be ineffective if all or most of the banks decided to expand, and each kept in step with the others. We come next to an argument introduced by Mountifort Longfield,[42] denying the force of the mechanism, even in the case of an expansion by only one bank. He illustrates the argument by an arithmetical example. Let us suppose that there are two banks, A and B,[43] who both carry on the same kind of business, all of which consists in lending by way of the issue of notes. Suppose also that in the initial period of

---

[41] *Op. cit.,* p. 70.

[42] He wrote a series of four articles on "Banking and Currency" in the *Dublin University Magazine* in 1840. The argument referred to comes in the second of these articles (February, 1840).

[43] A and B may be equally well taken to denote two *groups* of banks, one of which is conservative and the other expansive.

time A and B did the same amount of business and held equal gold reserves, so that in each case—

$$\text{Note issue} \quad = £40,000$$
$$\text{Gold reserve} = £15,000$$

and every week each bank discounts £10,000 in bills and receives the same amount in repayment of previous discounts. We may assume the repayments to each bank to be made partly in its own notes and partly in the notes of the other bank, the proportions being roughly the same as the proportions the separate note issues of the two banks bear to the total circulation. In this situation bank A will receive each week 5,000 of its own notes and 5,000 of B's, and B will receive the same, so that the daily or weekly exchanges of notes will just balance with no transfer of gold from the reserve of one bank to the reserve of the other. Now suppose that bank A decides to lend £20,000 more and increases its issues for this purpose by the same amount while B maintains the old position. Then, in the new situation, the proportion between the note issues of the two banks has changed from 1:1 to 3:2, and B will receive 6,000 of A's notes and 4,000 of its own notes, and it will return in the week 6,000 of A's notes to A. But since A's business now exceeds B's business in the proportion of 3:2 also, A will discount weekly, and therefore have falling due for payment in any week, bills to the extent of £15,000, of which £9,000 will be paid in its own notes and £6,000 in B's notes, so that it also has to return to B 6,000 notes. Thus the clearing account still gives no debit or credit on either side and no gold will be transferred. Consequently, B has no automatic check on A's expansion.

At a later stage the public starts demanding gold, however, and this demand will fall on the two banks in proportion to their shares of the total circulation. Suppose that the total demand is £20,000,[44] then in the final position A will have

$$\text{Note issue} \quad - \; £48,000,$$
$$\text{Gold reserve} = £3,000,$$

and B will have

$$\text{Note issue} \quad = \; £32,000,$$
$$\text{Gold reserve} = £7,000.$$

Thus the gold reserve of the bank which did not increase its circulation has been diminished in greater ratio than its circulation, and if the managers wish to keep the same reserve proportion as before (viz., 15:40) they must reduce their discounts "from £40,000 to about £30,000." "Hence a bank of issue may have its gold drained off by a rival which, if it has capital enough, may even ruin its competitor. If to avoid this calamity it contracts its issues, it thereby enables its rival to extend its business still more, until at last the more moderate bank is obliged to give up business altogether. Thus a bank may be driven in self-defence to take up the system of overtrading adopted by its competitors, and where there are several joint stock banks of issue, the country will suffer under alterations of high and low prices, of confidence and panic, of great excitement and general depression of trade. That bank will gain most which does most business during the period of excitement and is quickest and most resolute in contracting its issues and refusing to discount when the panic is coming. A system can scarcely be devised more injurious to the prosperity of a great commercial nation than this of permitting everybody who wishes it to make and issue that which is to be its circulating medium at the same time that it is their interest to issue as much as possible when the spirit of overtrading is prevalent and to reduce

---

[44] Longfield assumes that the circulation must fall back to the previous level; but this makes no difference to the main argument.

their issues when trade begins to stagnate and wants a stimulus to revive it."

Longfield's general conclusion is therefore the same as MacCulloch's, that far from the expanding bank being at the mercy of the conservative bank the latter is at the mercy of the former; there exists no automatic check on over-issues; on the contrary, rivalry among the banks leads to general expansion.

The point raised by the Longfield argument is by far the most important controversial point in the theory of free banking. No attempt was made in subsequent literature to reply to it, and we shall postpone the detailed examination of its validity until our final chapter.

We have tried in what precedes to connect together a series of rather disconnected remarks. There had been no organised discussion of the free-banking question by itself. There was all along a tendency in this country to accept the Bank of England's position and to concentrate attention on the banking and currency controversy and the general problem of central bank organisation. Probably the first discussion of the advantages of free competition that was anything like systematic was that given by James Wilson, first editor of *The Economist*, in a series of articles he published in that journal between 1845 and 1847.[45] When these articles were written the final decision against free entry into the note-issuing business had already been made in the Bank Act of 1844, and they are, as a not unnatural consequence, more an attempt to point out the nature and the origin of the system that had by this time become established, rather than to make recommendations for the adoption of an alternative system, and their main object was to denounce the theories of the currency school.

The privilege and monopoly of the Bank of England is, in

---

[45] Published also in book form, "Capital, Currency and Banking," 1847.

Wilson's opinion, the cause of England's lag behind Scotland, especially in the development of deposit business.[46] The more secure basis of, and the greater confidence of the public in, the Scottish banks was the outcome of the eminently satisfactory working of free competition. There had never been any restriction in Scotland on the number of partners allowed to combine to form a banking firm, and even before the advent of the joint stock company the firms had always consisted of a large number of known and wealthy men. "There can be no doubt," he says, "that were it not for the legal restrictions as to the formation of banks for the purpose of protecting the monopoly of the Bank of England, numerous large and wealthy joint stock banks would have been called into existence in the metropolis as well as in the provinces years ago, and would thus have prevented the establishment of those inferior banks, the failure of which from time to time has caused so much distress and ruin."[47]

He asks the question why it is that whereas the public and the legislature are content to allow free trade in deposit banking, they did not consider it a safe practice to give permission to issue notes payable on demand. The reason the currency school usually gave for this distinction was that bank notes increased the circulation and deposits did not. Such an argument was not, of course, acceptable to Wilson as a member of the banking school of thought which both denied that the issue of notes could be increased to any undesirable extent so long as convertibility was strictly maintained, and pointed out that the difference claimed between notes and deposit liabilities was invalid. But it was still denied in many quarters that demand deposits formed part of the circulation, and it was probably by no means generally admitted right up to the time of MacLeod.[48]

[46] See Article III.
[47] "Capital, Currency and Banking," p. 282.
[48] "Theory and Practice of Banking," 1855.

The events of 1847 led Wilson to an analysis of causes of commercial crises. He was clear that the nature of capital implied a choice between applying labour to produce implements which could be used for production in the future, and applying it to the production of goods immediately consumable in the present. His theory of the trade cycle is bound up with the distinction he draws between *fixed* and *floating* capital.[49] He was somewhat confused about the way in which fixed and floating capital were replaced from the income of the community and about the relation of all these variables to the fund for employing labour; he was under the impression that fixed capital is never returned.

It is rather remarkable that it should be the banking school who should first give support to the theory that it is the over-production of fixed capital which leads to booms and depressions.[50] A similar theory was held also by Bonamy

[49] "It is . . . not difficult to see that it becomes a most essential thing to the continued prosperity of a country that its *floating* capital, on which the continued reproduction of commodities of everyday use depends, as well as the continuous employment of labour, should not be withdrawn from those necessary purposes and converted into *fixed* capital in a greater degree than the surplus accumulation of the country, after replacing the whole fund needful to continue the production of such commodities . . . will admit. If the *floating* capital of the country is thus misdirected into *fixed* capital, it is quite plain that the ultimate result must be, that as the labour employed in the works representing the *fixed* capital does not reproduce the commodities which are consumed in supporting it, or any commodity which can be exchanged either with the home or foreign producers of such commodities, they must become scarce and dear, and ultimately the fund for the employment of labour must be diminished.

"It is quite true that for a time, while the process of the conversion of *floating* into *fixed* capital was proceeding, there would be a momentary appearance of great prosperity. . . . The production of commodities required for daily use would be unequal to the consumption; they would continue to rise in price. . . . The ultimate effect of such a disturbance or misdirection of the *floating* capital of the country would be to create a great scarcity of it which will be evinced by the high rate of interest." (*Op. cit.*, pp. 127–8.)

[50] Speaking of the railway development and the conversion of floating capital into fixed which this entailed, Wilson says that it is clear that "the first effect of this process would be to render capital scarce and in proportion to raise the rate of interest; and that the next effect would be by rendering commodities of consumption scarce, to increase their demand, and to afford thus a stronger

Price, and we shall notice it yet again when we come to the contributions made by Horn, in France. But the banking school did not, of course, connect up their theory with inflation as the root cause: this was left for a much later member of the currency school to do.[51]

From Wilson's time onwards for more than a decade the free-banking question was dropped in England, while on the Continent it was just beginning to gather force. So we turn now to France.

---

inducement to continue capital in its existing channel than to divert it into a new one." The inevitable result would be that a great majority of the railway schemes must be abandoned (*op. cit.*, p. 148).

[51] Viz., Geyer. See Chapter IX.

CHAPTER VIII

The Discussions
in France
and Belgium

At about the time when the issue in England had already been decided and the discussion had practically ceased, the controversy was just beginning to take shape in France. The slow development of banking facilities in France, particularly as compared with America, was first given literary emphasis by Michel Chevalier,[1] who was travelling in America between 1833 and 1835, just at a time when the whole banking question was foremost in the public mind in that country. Chevalier himself upheld the retention of the United States Bank, and suggested that France would greatly benefit by adopting a system of banks linked together like the twenty-five branches of the Bank of the United States.[2] Chevalier's remarks on the backward state of French banking were endorsed also by Carey, who testified to the beneficial effects of free competition. But an exactly opposite impression of the effects of freedom was created in France by Condy Raguet, and the translator[3] of his book in-

---

[1] "Lettres sur l'Amérique du Nord," 1836. "A long time must elapse before we can enjoy in France a system of credit as extensive as that which exists in England and the United States. We are in that respect in a state of barbarism" (Vol. II., p. 248).

[2] *Op. cit.*, Letter IV.

[3] Translated under the title "Traité des banques et de la circulation," by L. Lemaitre, 1840.

voked it in evidence of the evils that were wrought by competition in banking and of the superiority of a restrictive system like that of France.

All attempts at this time to state the rationale of the monopoly in the note issue had recourse to the State's exclusive right to the coining of money. This was an attitude taken up by Cieszkowski in a book[4] purporting to deal with the theory of money and credit, but containing, in fact, very little material of theoretical value. Non-note-issuing banks may, he says, be left free from legislative interference, but the right to issue notes is the right to coin money and must be either exercised or controlled by the State. The reasons he gives are almost purely juristic.[5] This appeal to the royal prerogative was to remain for many years the chief argument of the restrictionist school in France.

The agitation for greater freedom in the banking trade began with a pamphlet written by Courcelle-Seneuil in 1840.[6] The discussion became more important after the presentation of the report to the Senate in that same year on the project for the renewal of the privilege of the Bank of France and the debates on this report. The rapporteur, Rossi, gave a very gloomy picture of the effects of competition in the issue of paper money, and denied emphatically that there was any similarity between the application of free trade to industry and its application to the issue of bank notes. He gave his support to the retention of the old system of a single bank for each locality,[7] claiming at the same time that this was the only way of overcoming the French public's "bank shyness."

After this the free-banking party became more prominent. Coquelin, one of the leading members of the free trade asso-

---

[4] "Du Crédit et de la Circulation," 1839.
[5] *Op. cit.*, Chapter III.
[6] "Le Crédit et la Banque."
[7] Quoted by Wolowski, "La Question des Banques," pp. 192, 176 ff.

ciation and an economist of some repute at that time in France, wrote several articles[8] in its support and followed them up by a book.[9] His argument was based largely on the theory that economic crises are caused by restrictions on the investment of funds in bank capital, an argument to which we have referred already in connection with Carey. A more general and comprehensive statement of the case came from Courcelle-Seneuil,[10] whose ideas had been much influenced by the writings of James Wilson. He tries to justify his conclusions in favour of free banking by an attempt to show that over-issues of notes are not the cause of crises,[11] and that if banks make mistakes, it is never in their issues but always in their investments. He was in favour of absolute freedom and unlimited competition and was the most uncompromising of all the free bankers in France. The sole permissible regulation, in his view, was one aimed simply at the prevention of fraud. The distinction made between deposit banks and note-issuing banks, by which freedom was tolerated for the former but denied to the latter, was, in his opinion, all the more absurd when regard was had to the fact that the deposit liabilities of any bank are usually less widely spread over large numbers of people than its note liabilities; the failure to repay deposits might cause more harm than the failure to cash notes, because default in paying back deposits was likely to bring complete ruin to sev-

---

[8] See an article entitled "D'une Réforme du Régime Monétaire en France" in *La Revue des Deux Mondes*, Vol. III., (1844).

[9] "Du Crédit et des Banques," 1848.

[10] "Traité Théorique et Pratique des Operations de Banque," 1852.

[11] A view that was also supported later (1862) by Juglar in his "Des Crises Commerciales et leur Retour Périodique en France, en Angleterre et aux Etats-Unis," in which, while noting the marked correlation between the increase in the volume of discounts and of the note issue on the one hand, and in prices and the diminution of the metallic reserves on the other, he regards such movements as the results of other underlying factors rather than as the causes; he says: "Les excès de l'émission ne sont pas la cause principale des crises" (p. 34).

eral families, whereas in the case of notes the loss would be distributed among large numbers of people.

The free-banking position was also supported by Du Puynode, another adherent of the trade cycle theory of Carey and Coquelin. In common with the majority of the free bankers in France he favoured the allowance of limited liability. He looked upon the unlimited liability provisions of the English law as the chief fault of the English banking system, claiming that they had actually caused the total security given by the shareholders to the note-holders and depositors to be smaller than it would be under limited liability.[12]

Interest in the subject was greatly increased when the Bank of France raised the rate of discount early in 1857, and the discussion was soon attracting the attention of most of the better-known writers on economic subjects of the day. The circle which it interested was much wider than in England, where exceedingly few of the academic economists touched on the subject. In France it was, among economists, the leading controversy of the time. In 1857 it was taken up by the *Société d'Economie Politique*, at whose meetings both the general question of the limitation of note issues,[13] and the specific subject of *"La Liberté des Banques,"*[14] were debated among a group which included Wolowski, Chevalier, Horn, Joseph Garnier, Courcelle-Seneuil, Paul Coq and Léonce de Lavergne.

Garnier spoke against all intervention of authority and all administrative supervision in banking, but Chevalier was not so unreservedly in favour of entirely withdrawing all intervention. He declared that he was not prepared to go so far as to demand a *régime* of complete liberty for institutions of

[12] "De la Monnaie, du Crédit et de L'Impôt," 1853, p. 237.

[13] See the report in *La Revue des Deux Mondes*, 2me série, Vol. XXI., (1857), p. 471.

[14] See the report in *Le Journal des Economistes*, 2me série, Vol. XIV., (May, 1857).

issue and credit, and this was regarded by the restrictionist school as an important admission from one of the promoters of free trade in France.[15]

The next important contributions were called out in response to the propaganda writings of anonymous pamphleteers[16] in connection with the Bank of Savoy affair and the attack on the Bank of France,[17] and by 1864 the controversy was at its height.

The counter-attack on the pamphlets and on the general question of plurality, even of the most restricted variety, was opened by Victor Bonnet.[18] Generalising from the case of the old departmental banking system he concluded that if there are a number of banks, the notes of each bank do not circulate beyond a certain locality. Anybody who wants to make payment in another locality has to procure notes issued by a bank in that locality and has therefore to submit to the same inconveniences and extra trouble as he does in buying foreign exchange to make payments to another country. The advantage of having a single note issuer is that all this is avoided, because the notes of this issuer circulate everywhere within the country. Bonnet gave this as the reason why the people had been far more willing to accept notes, and the total circulation had extended, since the suppression of the departmental banks. This argument against a plural system was really quite valueless, because it ignores the circumstance that the departmental banks had been de-

---

[15] He was the French negotiator and therefore Cobden's counterpart in the 1860 Commercial Treaty between France and England.

[16] "Réorganisation des Banques: Légalité et Urgence d'une Réforme," 1861; "Réorganisation du système des banques: Banque de France, Banque de Savoie," 1863, both ascertained later to have been written by the Pereire brothers.

[17] See also Gustave Marqfoy, "La Banque de France dans ses rapports avec le crédit et la circulation," 1862, in which it is contended that it is the duty of the Bank of France to keep the price of credit invariable by counteracting by its own lending any tendency to a rise in the rate of interest on the market.

[18] "La Liberté des Banques d'Emission et le Taux de L'Interêt" in *La Revue des Deux Mondes*, Tome XLIX., January 1st, 1864.

prived by law of all the normal mechanisms for the interchange of notes. He repeated also the argument used in England after the crisis of 1825 that if there are several banks, the solidarity of one tends to depend on that of the others, and if there is a run on one, the others will also be affected to a greater or lesser degree; if, on the contrary, there is one bank like the Bank of France, the public has much more confidence in it, panics are avoided and the whole credit system is thereby rendered more stable.

On the other side, the attack on the Bank of France was resumed by Isaac Pereire.[19] He denounced the policy of raising the rate of discount as a means of protecting the metallic reserves and suggested that the proper method of procedure was first for the bank to realise its capital, and then if the effect of doing this were insufficient, to augment its capital; the resources obtained would enable it to buy the gold necessary for the specie reserve. He denied, in the second place,[20] that there was any necessity for the Bank of France to raise her rate when a neighbouring country (*e.g.*, England) did the same. In his opinion the rate of discount should be invariable at 3 percent.[21] Much the same attitude was taken by Maurice Aubry,[22] a Paris banker. There is no better example than this book of Aubry's of the influence active ever since the time of Napoleon,[23] not only in France but also in Germany, of the doctrine that the chief function of banks of issue is to keep the rate of discount down, a doctrine which, when adopted as a rule of bank policy, was

[19] "La Banque de France et l'Organisation du Crédit en France" (1864).

[20] *Op. cit.*, p. 40.

[21] *Op. cit.*, p. 73.

[22] "Les Banques d'Emission et d'Escompte" (1864).

[23] The low discount rate school in France made frequent reference to the words of Napoleon written to his Minister of Finance, Mollien, in 1808: "Ce que vous devez dire au gouverneur de la Banque et aux régents, c'est qu'ils doivent écrire *en lettres d'or* dans le livre de leurs assemblées ces mots: Quel est le *but* de la Banque de France? D'escompter les crédits *de toutes les maisons de commerce à* 4%."

bound to lead to credit inflations. Aubry bases his attack on the Bank of France on the grounds that the privilege of note issue was given to the bank solely in order to favour cheap discount,[24] and it was therefore highly improper for it to charge a high rate; and in this respect it was in an entirely different position from that of the Bank of England, since whereas the latter might legitimately use the rate of discount to control movements of specie, the Bank of France could not do so because it was its declared duty to keep the rate of interest low.[25] So he, also, recommends an alternative policy of calling on the shareholders to supply additional capital in times of crisis and paying it back as soon as there is no further need for it.[26]

Pereire was by no means in favour of general freedom of entry into the note-issuing business.[27] He limited his demands to one rival establishment to break the monopoly of the Bank of France,[28] the substitution of a duopoly for a monopoly.

Aubry wanted the monopoly retained, and seemingly for no better reason than that the coining of money, and therefore the issue of bank-notes, was a royal prerogative,[29] a proposition that was, according to him, one of the fundamental axioms of political economy. It was pointed out a little later by Etienne Duran[30] that it was as a result of the application of the royal prerogative to the issue of paper money that most countries had had their most fatal experiences of paper money, and it was a grave mistake to reproach free banking with the errors of which the royal prerogative had been the sole cause.

[24] *Op. cit.*, p. 10.
[25] *Op. cit.*, pp. 127–8.
[26] *Op. cit.*, pp. 172–3.
[27] *Op. cit.*, p. 6.
[28] *Op. cit.*, p. 115.
[29] *Op. cit.*, p. 55.
[30] "Encore la Question des Banques," 1865.

The idea of free banking had raised in many people's minds the vision of anybody and everybody becoming note issuers, and they saw insuperable difficulties in the circulation of the notes of innumerable bankers and feared that unsound firms would have a positive encouragement to set up under the shadow of the multiplicity of different notes, and the practical impossibility of the public being able to exercise a close scrutiny over all the notes they accepted. It was along these lines that the case for unity in the note issue was formulated by those among the restrictionists who succeeded in getting away from the purely political argument of the royal prerogative. Thus it was argued by Adolphe d'Eichtal[31] that the State intervened to assure the public of guarantees because the holder of a note was almost never in a position to know the real position of the debtor,[32] and unity in the note issue avoided the inconveniences of having to examine each note carefully to see if it was issued by a bank that was likely to be able to pay it or by one that was not likely to be in that position.

A Belgian economist[33] of the free-banking school pointed out[34] in reply to this line of argument, that the danger that "men of straw" would be able to obtain acceptance for their notes was much diminished when it was realised that the supervision of issues would become largely a matter for the bankers themselves. It was not to be expected that the public would exercise no scrutiny at all, and it was a reasonable assumption to make that the trader would willingly accept the notes of his own banker and the notes of such other banks as his own banker was also willing to receive. This was, of course, only a very partial solution of that particular difficulty which referred to the unduly heavy pressure of

[31] "De la Monnaie de Papier et des Banques d'Emission," 1864.
[32] *Op. cit.,* p. 13.
[33] Brasseur.
[34] "Manuel d'Economie Politique," Vol. II., 1864, p. 277.

insolvencies on the small note-holder, who was unlikely to come into contact with the banks as a customer.

The case for competition was also taken up by Paul Coq, Mannequin and Chevalier. Paul Coq[35] endorsed the views of the Pereire brothers that the rate of discount charged by the Bank of France had risen as soon as, and because, the destruction of the departmental banks had given it an unrestricted monopoly of the note issue. Mannequin's contribution[36] was simply a defence of free banking against the allegation that it would lead to over-issue on the usual lines of the banking school, that so long as the notes "are not thrown out of the window," but are issued only in response to the needs of trade, they cannot be issued in excess. Chevalier was responsible for bringing the subject to the notice of a wide circle of readers by his contributions to the newspapers, notably to the *Journal des Débats*. Courcelle-Seneuil also re-expounded his views in the *Journal des Economistes.*[37]

A publication which provoked a good deal of discussion was an article by Léonce de Lavergne,[38] in which he proposed to replace the monopoly of the Bank of France not by completely free competition but by a limited plurality. He said it was impossible to manage a large area from one centre as the Bank of France was trying to do, and an adequate provision of banking offices could best be provided by a system of eight or ten regions, each having its parent bank with branches. This was a plea for something similar to the old departmental banks but without the old restrictions.

[35] Article "Les Banques de France et de Savoie," in the *Journal des Economistes*, 2me série, Vol. 121., January, 1864. See also his book, "Les Circulations en Banque ou l'Impasse du Monopole, Emission et Change," 1865.

[36] Article "De la Liberté des Banques" in the above number of *Le Journal des Economistes.*

[37] Articles on "La Liberté des Banques" in the *Journal des Economistes*, 1864 and 1865.

[38] "La Banque de France et les Banques Départementales" in *La Revue des Deux Mondes*, April 15th, 1864.

Probably the most influential disputants were Wolowski and Chevalier, who were on opposite sides in the controversy and undertook a direct discussion and exchange of views. Wolowski had begun his career as a lawyer, and his arguments were characteristically based on juristic rather than economic reasoning. Chevalier had been in his earlier years, before going to America, associated with the Pereire brothers in the Saint-Simonian movement. Although his arguments were much less specious than those of the Pereires, we find him again by their side in this discussion supporting the main tenets of their position. There is no doubt that all three carried with them in their later days the ideas of the Saint-Simonians on banking and credit. In the newly constructed society envisaged by the Saint-Simonians the bank was to play a great directing and centralising role. The banks were to be responsible for estimating the quality and quantity of the needs of the community for capital, and for this purpose there were to be large numbers of them specialising in the separate industries and linked up to a central bank. The outer banks were to inform the central bank of the circumstances of their localities and industries, and the central bank was to distribute the credits between them. In all discussions of the plan great emphasis was placed on the importance of credit facilities and of the wide dispersion of agencies for the distribution of credit.[39]

As a member first of the Chamber of Deputies and later of the Senate, Chevalier had plenty of opportunity of attracting public attention to his views. He adopted the attitude[40] that since free trade and all that *laisser-faire* principles implied was now the accepted policy, since the era of monopolies was said to have passed and competition was regarded as

[39] See J. B. Vergeot, "Le Crédit comme Stimulant et Régulateur de l'Industrie—La conception saint-simonniene, ses réalisations, son application au problème bancaire d'après-guerre."

[40] Letter in *Le Journal des Débats*, February 4th, 1864.

being beneficial to the community, the burden of the proof
of the contention that the same system was not applicable to
banking was on those who asserted it and not on those who
denied it; because on the face of it those who oppose free
banking oppose also freedom to build railways, and free exchange in general, which, as he knew, they did not do, and
he insisted that they had as yet given no sufficient reason for
the attitude they took towards banking. Wolowski took up
the other side in a book[41] of extensive proportions, which
contained, however, no very original additions to what had
already been said on the subject. It was almost wholly a repetition of the views expressed by others and a commentary
on the trend of policy already adopted in the matter. But his
doctrinal importance in the French developments must not
be under-estimated, for he stood out among the French
school as the most emphatic adherent of the use of the rate
of discount as a means of controlling specie flows.

This brings us to the eve of the French *Banque Enquête*.[42]
The enquiry arose out of the Bank of Savoy affair and the
raising of the rate of discount in 1864, and was entrusted to
the *Conseil supérieur de l'agriculture du commerce et des
travaux publics*, of which both Chevalier and d'Eichtal were
members, and therefore took part in the examination of
witnesses. The report is contained in six volumes and com-
prises altogether close on five thousand pages. The Council
called as witnesses, besides the delegates from the Bank of
France, all those who had gained anything of a reputation as
writers on subjects connected with money and banking. A
number of foreign economists were also invited to state their
views, and written memoranda were submitted by Thomson
Hankey, William Newmarch, R. H. Patterson and J. S. Mill,
from England, Professor de Laveleye, from Belgium, and Pro-

[41] "La Question des Banques," 1864.
[42] "Enquête sur les principes et les faits généraux qui régissent la circulation
monétaire et fiduciaire," 1865–66.

fessor Tellkampf, from Germany. In addition, Walter Bagehot had the distinction of being called as first witness before the Commission. Among the French witnesses some had already published their views (e.g. Wolowski, Isaac Pereire, Bonnet, d'Eichtal, Aubry, Lavergne, Chevalier, Courcelle-Seneuil, Paul Coq), and we shall have occasion to refer to others (Cernuschi, Coullet, and Horn), who were writing contemporaneously with the enquiry. Looked at as a whole, the evidence cannot be said to have contained any considerable amount of material of value from the point of view of monetary theory. Chevalier made clear his views on the subject of discount policy in the course of his examination of the representatives of the Bank of France. He doubted the utility or the necessity of using the rate of discount or even the restriction of credit in general, no matter what the means, as a remedy for stopping a gold efflux.[43] The policy that was, in his opinion, the correct one, was that of the sale of its "rentes" by the Bank,[44] and he emphasised the necessity of not immobilising the capital of the bank in quasi-irredeemable Government obligations which might not be available for this purpose. What Chevalier, along with the other supporters of the same policy, such as Aubry and the Pereires, overlooked, was that the sale of securities by the Bank must contract credit just as certainly as a direct contraction of the amount of bills discounted by the Bank. It would deprive the short-term loan market of the amount of funds acquired by the Bank for the securities it sold, and so there must be a tendency for loan rates to rise. This school thought they had discovered an ingenious device in the shape of an open market operation which would make the Bank more liquid without causing stringency in the money market.

More careful attention was by this time being given to the

[43] "Dépositions de MM. les délégués et les régents de la Banque de France," pp. 81–117.
[44] *Op. cit.*, p. 112.

comparative effect of the alternative systems on the total volume of money and credit. Up to now the free bankers had by no means been of identical opinion. Some of them had held that there was no reason inherent in the free-banking system why its issue should be more expansive than the issue of a central banking system. Others had argued that a free-banking system had a positive advantage in replacing a large part of metallic money by fiduciary money which, costing nothing, could be lent cheaply and thus favour the development of trade and industry. The ideas of this school were openly inflationary and provoked the attack of a number of people who took up an anti-inflationist attitude.

Emile de Laveleye, a Belgian Professor of Political Economy, attacked[45] the expansionist section of the free-banking school on two grounds. Firstly, he said that if what they claimed, namely, that free banking would lead to an expansion of the circulation, was true, this must be followed by a heavy drain on bank reserves of specie followed by a contraction of the circulation, and a crisis. He pointed out that the crisis would be, moreover, of greater violence under a system of a large number of banks as compared with the case of a privileged bank which, having the unlimited confidence of the public, could extend its issues at such times. But in the second place, de Laveleye argued that the free bankers might be wrong in assuming that their system would provide easier credit conditions in the upward swing of the cycle, and that it was, on the contrary, conceivable that it would involve the keeping of larger reserves than the present system and therefore would lead actually to a smaller circulation. He was himself willing to consider the free-banking system on condition that the banks should be subjected to the condition of unlimited liability.

Just at this time there began an attack on bank-notes in

---

[45] "Le Marché Monétaire et ses Crises depuis Cinquante Ans," 1865.

general. It was opened by Cernuschi,[46] who held that the vital question was not one of whether the note issue should be in the hands of a few or of many banks, but whether banknotes should be issued at all. They had the effect of spoliating the holders of metallic money by depreciating its value, and if they had any use at all they should be made to represent mere certificates for gold deposited and the fiduciary or uncovered issue should cease entirely. But he joined in the demand for free banking because he thought that if any and every bank were allowed to issue notes, nobody would accept them any longer, and so they would disappear. The same attitude towards the bank-note was taken up by Modeste.[47] Courcelle-Seneuil, Du Puynode and Mannequin entered the discussion on the other side.[48]

Perhaps the best analysis of the point of view of the central banking school was that made by Coullet.[49] He sets out the advantages and disadvantages of each of the alternative systems, and decides that the weight of the argument is in favour of monopoly and centralisation. He defends the distinction commonly made between notes on the one hand, and bills of exchange and deposits on the other, because of the element of compulsion in the acceptance of the former and the fact that it is not the people who are enabled to borrow on easier terms and so benefit by the extension of the banks' issues who are likely to suffer when the notes depreciate, since the notes will by this time have passed into the hands of third parties.[50]

---

[46] "Mécanique de l'échange," 1865, and "Contre le Billet de Banque," 1865, the latter being the evidence he gave before the Banque Enquête.

[47] "Le Billet des Banques d'Emission et la Fausse Monnaie" in *Le Journal des Economistes*, Vol. III., August 15th, 1866.

[48] Courcelle-Seneuil, "Le Billet de Banque n'est pas Fausse Monnaie" in the same journal, September 15th, 1866. See also a letter by Du Puynode in the same number, a reply by Modeste in the October number and an article by Mannequin in the December number.

[49] "Etudes sur la Circulation Monétaire," 1865.

[50] *Op. cit.*, pp. 78–80: "Les billets à ordre et les lettres de change les effets de

Coullet believed that freedom of issue would accomplish its own destruction, and was, therefore, in a somewhat similar though not so extreme position as Cernuschi. He supposed that as the result of the numerous failures that were bound to occur under such a system one of two things would happen: *either* the public, struck by the contrast between the majority of the banks and a few or even perhaps a single bank, would in future confine its dealings to these or this bank and so there would be established a *de facto* monopoly, *or* the whole system would be afflicted and the bank-note would be abandoned altogether. If, however, it should prove possible to build up a system of well-organised and solid banks, the result (he thought) of plurality would be not a lowering of the rate of interest but a raising of the rate, because of the anxiety of the banks (even in normal times) to keep adequate reserves. Even in ordinary times, and against the same total circulation, the united reserves of a large number of banks would have to be greater than the total reserves of a single bank. Moreover, the centralisation of reserves had an advantage as a source of strength in periods of crisis. The advantages of monopoly were, in Coullet's opinion, more than sufficient to outweigh the avowed danger of the Government's abusing its power over the single bank of issue.

commerce proprement dits, les promesses de payer à une date fixe et à une personne désignée, ne peuvent circuler, nous l'avons démontré, qu'entre individus qui se connaissent, il y a examen du titre cédé, discussion de sa valeur, endos, garantie nouvelle et additionelle donnée par le cédant au cessionnaire. . . . Quand ces promesses demeurent impayées à l'échéance, les détenteurs se reprochent à eux-mêmes leur imprévoyance ou leur peu d'aptitude aux affaires. . . . Ce que nous disons des effets de commerce ordinaires peut s'appliquer exactement aux dépôts chez les banquiers. Nulle raison générale ne pousse les particuliers à faire le dépôt de leurs fonds chez un autre. Le choix parfaitement libre d'un dépositaire est toujours déterminé par des considérations individuelles. . . . Si les billets à vue et au porteur ne circulaient comme les autres effets de commerce que dans un petit nombre de mains, si leur transmission pouvait être précédé d'un examen détaillée et accompagnée d'une garantie du cédant au cessionaire, les pouvoirs publics n'auraient pas à intervenir pour les réglementer. . . . Mais chacun sait qu'il n'en est point ainsi."

The best exposition of the free-banking case came from J. E. Horn.[51] In the first place he disposed of the royal prerogative argument in economic terms.[52] While pointing out that it was private industry that had first commenced the coinage of specie, he submitted that there were probably two reasons why it had later been taken over as a State monopoly and claimed as a royal right. One was in order to facilitate the circulation of coins as a medium of exchange over wide areas at a time when the State was the only institution that was generally enough known to inspire sufficient confidence that the coins were what they professed to be in weight and fineness, and so to make it unnecessary to weigh and assay every coin before accepting it. The second reason was that the King found it the most convenient way of acquiring revenue. In our day, he continues, however, it is no longer necessary as a budgetary source,[53] and neither is it true any more that the State is the only institution which could provide the service of coinage. If a firm like Rothschild, in Paris, or Baring, in London, were to undertake the stamping of coins, they would be just as willingly accepted as the coin of the realm.

Horn, in company with Chevalier and Courcelle-Seneuil, and also many of the less prominent writers on free banking, denied that bank-notes were money, and this became one of the major issues between these writers and Wolowski. It was an attitude which was, of course, in many cases adopted, perhaps rather unnecessarily, merely in order to bring bank-notes outside the prerogative of the Crown in the coinage of money, and was little more than the playing off of sophistry against sophistry. A great deal of space was devoted to this discussion of a matter which was, in the last

---

[51] "La Liberté des Banques," 1866.

[52] *Op. cit.*, p. 62.

[53] It would still, even in our day, seem that the note issue is of the utmost importance as a budgetary source in time of war.

analysis, a question of definition as to whether two things should be denoted by the same term because they possessed a certain characteristic in common, or whether they should be sharply contrasted because they differed in respect of a second characteristic. Wolowski was defining bank-notes as money because both bank-notes and coin exert like effects on trade and prices. Chevalier and the others were insisting on the necessity for always regarding bank-notes as merely substitutes for, and always convertible into, coin, since any view which neglected the condition of strict convertibility must lead to their over-issue and unlimited depreciation.

Turning to the positive disadvantages of a privileged monopoly, Horn called attention to the greater possibility that the liability of such a bank to pay out specie on demand would be revoked with its consequence of pure paper money in place of notes convertible into coin. A bank under State patronage always counted on the Government to relieve it of its obligation to pay when nearing insolvency, and its bankruptcy became legalised instead of its having to go into liquidation and suffer the usual penalties of insolvency. The history of privileged banks had undeniably been full of bankruptcies. If banks of issue were given to understand, however, that they were positively and irremediably responsible for their acts, and had themselves to bear the consequences, they would be as prudent in their policy as any other business concern.[54] There was also, as Chevalier[55] had already emphasised, the ever-present temptation for the Government to abuse its power over the privileged bank.

There can be no guarantee that failures will never occur under either system, but in the case of a plural system only the notes of the failed firms depreciate, whereas in the case

[54] *Op. cit.*, p. 396.

[55] "On a porté l'abus à ce point, que la facilité d'émission dont les banques étaient investies fut pour le gouvernement la planche aux assignats; de là résultait bientôt l'insolvabilité de la banque." Quoted by Wolowski, "La Banque d'Angleterre," p. 199.

of a privileged monopoly the legalised suspension, and therefore the depreciation, affects the whole of the note issue. Moreover, if banks temporarily suspended payments under a free system, the competition of banks still maintaining cash payments would wipe them out of business if they did not hasten to resume payments, and suspensions would therefore be of shorter duration.

Banking freedom in the true sense of the word, and the system which Horn favoured, was a system in which companies would be allowed to set up in the banking business, whether issue, discount or deposit, under just the same regulations as those under which companies were allowed to set up, in other industries,[56] regulations which concentrated on the prevention of fraud. But he permitted that it was not unreasonable that people should want to add to these stipulations some others specially relating to companies undertaking the issue of notes,[57] because of the circumstance that, in addition to the shareholders and the people who contract with the company, there is a third class involved, namely, the indirect and to a certain extent involuntary acceptors of bank-notes, and it was on these grounds that he thought the 1863 legislation of the United States was admissible. Such regulations, however, he still regarded as not entirely indispensable.

In sympathy with the tradition of the banking school, Horn was of the opinion that a crisis could never be caused by an over-issue of notes, since no more would get into circulation than just sufficed to satisfy a genuine demand. Banks, therefore, made mistakes not in the quantity of their issues but in the lines in which they made their investments, and crises were caused according to him by a scarcity of circulating capital. In periods of "over-investment" too much circulating capital is transformed into fixed capital un-

[56] *Op. cit.*, p. 392.
[57] *Op. cit.*, p. 414.

til it is discovered that there is an insufficiency of the auxiliary materials necessary to co-operate with it.[58]

The direct discussion between Wolowski and Chevalier continued for some years, and the correspondence was published by Wolowski in his later book.[59] Courcelle-Seneuil also made another final statement of his position,[60] again pointing out the extreme lack of banking facilities in the provinces in general, and of agricultural credit in particular. Neither Courcelle-Seneuil nor Horn was a member of that group of free bankers who supported their case because they expected it to increase the possibilities of expansion and the lowering of the rate of interest. Courcelle-Seneuil did not regard it as certain that issues would be greater under competition, nor that the rate of interest would be lowered, and in so far as the latter was at all likely he thought it would come, not by way of increased issues, but by way of the collection and utilisation of idle savings. He was the most unyielding of all the free bankers, insisting on complete liberty as understood in other branches of trade and industry. He refused to consider the application of any special regulations to the case of banking, and emphatically denied the favourite contention of the restrictionists[61] that banking firms, unlike those in other industries, cannot be made to bear themselves the consequences of their mistakes.

---

[58] *Op. cit.*, p. 125: "C'est l'huile qui manque pour graisser la machine, l'eau qui fait défaut pour alimenter la chaudière; toutes les entreprises s'en ressentiront; les plus solides marcheront avec difficulté; les moins forts s'arrêteront; les faibles s'éclateront."

[59] "La Banque d'Angleterre et les Banques d'Ecosse," 1857.

[60] "La Banque Libre; exposé des fonctions du commerce de banque et de son application à l'agriculture suivi de divers écrits de controverse sur la liberté des banques," 1867.

[61] "Ils raisonnent comme s'il était indifférent aux banques de faire faillite, c'est à dire comme si elles devaient être dirigées uniquement par des personnes décidées à faire une banqueroute frauduleuse. Il nous semble que les personnes de ce caractère, bien que trop nombreuses, sont une exception dans le monde commercial, et que ce ne sont pas celles qui commandent habituellement la confiance publique."

It will be remembered that in England, prior to 1844, it had been a constantly recurring complaint that the efforts of the Bank of England to contract credit in time of a specie outflow were always rendered nugatory by the failure of the country banks to do the same, and it was held up against the free note-issuing rights of these banks that they were insensitive to the foreign exchanges. This same argument was re-introduced in a slightly more sophisticated form by Clement Juglar.[62] He used it in favour of a certain type of centralisation. His argument ran that there was a practical difficulty in a plural system in distributing the demands for specie to send abroad because the settlement of commercial operations with foreign centres tends to concentrate in the large towns and the demands for specie will fall on the banks in these places, while others are unaffected by the drain on reserves and have no incentive to check their issues. From this he drew the inference that the best system would certainly be one that was free and competitive in the sense that there should be a large number of banks spread over all localities, but that it should be controlled from the centre by the Bank of France acting as a clearing-house. The chief purpose of his central bank was to render the banks lying outside the trading centres sensitive to the forces necessitating a contraction of the currency by facilitating clearing operations. But it is extremely doubtful whether any such externally imposed institution as the Bank of France or any other is necessary to effect these operations. With reasonable communications and no artificially imposed obstacles, clearing arrangements will be made by the banks themselves. Thus, if one group of banks (A) near the ports or in Paris is affected directly by gold withdrawals for export and contracts its note issue, but another group (B) is not so affected, group A

---

[62] "Du Change et de la Liberté d'Emission," 1868.

will have less notes in circulation in proportion to the circulation of B than it did before; the clearing balances will go in favour of A, who will consequently acquire claims on the gold reserves of B. This will constrain B to contract its liabilities and so the contraction will be diffused throughout the whole system. The difficulty raised by Juglar to a position of such primary importance was imaginary rather than real and would certainly not in itself provide the sole reason for the existence of institutions endowed with such privileges and position of ascendancy as the Bank of France. Juglar was really advocating a mixed system in which rights of issue should be given to the competitive banks, but in which there should be a central bank with a controlling influence, something between free banking in the pure sense and the single privileged monopoly system in vogue in France.

What is the connection between the free-banking school and the banking school, on the one hand, and between the central banking school and the currency school on the other? It is not unnatural to expect it to be very close in both cases. It is especially noticeable in France that most of the free bankers were adherents of the banking theory which denied that bank-notes could be over-issued so long as convertibility was maintained. Brasseur, Horn, Courcelle-Seneuil, Coq and Mannequin were among the most convinced of the banking theorists. Cernuschi was an exception. He was a member of the strictest section of the currency school which believed not merely that the fiduciary issue should be fixed, and any issue above this limit covered by metal, but that there should be no fiduciary circulation at all. He supported free banking, however, for the peculiar reason, as we have already explained, that he thought such a system would destroy the note issue altogether.

Adherence to the tenets of the central banking school correspondingly usually carried with it the support of the principles of the currency school. The exception in this case was Coullet, who opposed the fixing of any limits on the fiduciary issue so long as there was only one bank of issue.

Among those who opposed the unlimited right of issue of the Bank of France there began at this time a discussion of the relative merits of the fixed fiduciary issue and the fixed reserve proportion. The latter was a rather less rigid interpretation of the currency doctrine. Wolowski was a great admirer of Peel's Act, and Cernuschi also preferred this to the reserve proportion method of controlling issues for the reason that the latter tended to cause greater embarrassment in time of specie withdrawals, but Léonce de Lavergne and Adolphe d'Eichtal both favoured the second method.

By the beginning of the 'seventies the attention of monetary theorists had been turned to the bi-metallic question. Wolowski and Cernuschi both figured among the supporters of the retention of the double standard.

CHAPTER IX

The Discussions
in Germany

In Germany the question of banking freedom came to the forefront of discussion later even than in France. An early book that had some considerable influence was the account given by F. A. von Gerstner[1] of the impressions he gathered when travelling in America, and in which he attributed the swift development of American industry and commerce to the banks.[2] He was responsible for arousing a good deal of false optimism as to the effects of credit expansion, and led some readers to believe that banks were vested with a kind of magic power.

It was not until the 'fifties that any modern literature on banking and currency of any importance was written, and then within a few years three writers came into the foreground—Otto Hübner, J. L. Tellkampf and Adolf Wagner. The first of these, Hübner, was an active member of the German Free Trade Party. His book[3] consisted for the most part of a survey, largely historical and statistical, of the chief banking institutions then in existence all over the world. His

---

[1] "Bericht aus den Vereinigten Staaten Nord Amerika's über Eisenbahnen, Dampfschiffahrten, Banken und andere öffentliche Unternehmungen," 1839.

[2] "Drei Gegenstände sind es vorzüglich, welchen die Vereinigten Staaten ihren Wohlstand verdanken: die Schulen . . . ; die Banken, 800 an der Zahl, welche jedermann mit Leichtigkeit Geldmittel, seinem Vermögen angemessen, darbieten, und ihn in die Lage setzen, an Spekulationen jeder Art Theil zu nehmen: endlich Eisenbahnen, Canäle und Dampfschiffahrt. . . . " *Op. cit.*, p. 1.

[3] "Die Banken," 1854.

general conclusions were strongly in support of free banking. Practical experience had shown, he said, that banks were least often insolvent where they were least restricted.[4] States never gave privileges without demanding a *quid pro quo,* and if banks wanted to keep their privileges they had got to fulfil the wishes of the Government. "For exclusively privileged banks," he said, "insolvency is as a rule the entrepreneur's best speculation"; foremost in his mind was the case of the Austrian National Bank; without declaring itself insolvent it could never have lent such large sums to the Government, but if it had not lent the Government what it did, its profits would have been much smaller.[5] The contrast is between privileged banks which are protected by the law from the consequences of their mistakes (if they should become insolvent, the Government gives forced currency to their notes) and the free-banking system where the bankers must bear the results of their own acts. Moreover, the mere fact that the State supports a privileged bank gives it an unwarranted trust.

Hübner did not base his case for free banking on the theories of the banking school—on the contrary: he was the first of a group that became rather fashionable in Germany, that held that only so many notes should be issued as there was metal to back them.[6] The rule was that banks should not lend more than they receive. It followed that Hübner was also not a member of that division of the free-banking school which looked upon free banking as a means of lowering interest rates. If such a lowering of interest rates were to accompany an increase in the circulation, it would, he said, be an expression of the unhealthiness which such an increase produces.[7] If it were true that the State could be trusted al-

---

[4] *Op. cit.,* Vol. I., p. 32.
[5] *Op. cit.,* Vol. I., p. 33.
[6] *Op. cit.,* Vol. I., p. 73.
[7] *Op. cit.,* Vol. I., p. 73. "Die Papier ohne Metallhinlage, die Erhöhung der Preise aller Dinge, sind ein scheinbarer Vermögenszuwachs, der genossen und

ways only to issue notes to the amount of its specie holdings, a State-controlled note issue would be the best system,[8] but as things were, a far nearer approach to the ideal system was to be expected from free banks, who for reasons of self-interest would aim at the fulfilment of their obligations.

The same rigid interpretation of the currency doctrine found a second supporter in Tellkampf. In his earlier years he had travelled in America, and it was his observations of the abuses of the banking system in that country which were supposed to have led him to his conclusions that the amount of paper should be regulated strictly by the amount of specie deposited in exchange and that the issues should be in the hands of a single bank. He had published these views in America as early as 1842,[9] but they did not at that time attract much attention. Having returned to Germany he became Professor of Political Economy at Breslau and was also elected to membership of the Prussian Senate, where he took a leading part in the discussions on bank legislation. One of the points with which he was concerned in his first book[10] was to combat the idea still pervading some circles in Germany that banking possessed the power to effect unlimited increases in real wealth.[11] On the question of freedom he drew a sharp distinction between note-issuing and deposit banking. It was, in his view, impossible to allow the former to be carried on by all private persons without legal limitation, but he makes an exception to this rule under two conditions. Firstly, the issuers must be subjected to unlim-

---

verzehrt wird. Da dies Vermögen aber eben nur scheinbar, da es kein Kapital, kein ersparter Überschuss, ist, so wirkt sein verzehrter Betrag, schliesslich als ein Deficit zwischen Haben und Soll. Man hat keinen Vermögenszuwachs, sondern das alte Vermögen verzehrt."

[8] *Op. cit.*, Vol. I., p. 123.

[9] Hunt's "Merchants' Magazine and Commercial Review," Vol. IV., p. 70.

[10] "Über die Neuere Entwicklung des Bankwesens in Deutschland mit Hinweis auf dessen Vorbilder in England, Schottland und Nord-Amerika und auf die französische Société Générale du Crédit Mobilier," 1856.

[11] He attacks particularly von Gerstner's views.

ited liability. Limited liability was, he contended, not a right that could be demanded in the name of free trade but a privilege by the granting of which the State had undermined the natural principle of responsibility underlying free trade. Secondly, the note issuers must be free from all obligation to lend to the State.

While Tellkampf looked to centralisation of the note issue as the ultimate end to be sought,[12] there was at this time in Prussia no prospect of attaining any effective unity in the note issue, and the increase in the number of banks and their unlimited issues in the "Border States" led him to favour Prussia's setting up her own private banks so as to keep out the notes of these other States. He recommended that these new banks should be set up on the Scotch model,[13] on the principle that if the shareholders were liable for their obligations to the full extent of their property, self-interest would provide the necessary limitation on note issues.[14]

By far the best known among the German economists of his generation was Adolf Wagner. As strictly as Tellkampf was a follower of the currency tradition, Wagner was an adherent of the banking school. Writing at a time when the currency doctrine was becoming very powerful on the Continent, he set out in this first book[15] to do two things: The one was to explain the disadvantages from the economic point of view of the ruling system of privileged banks, and the other to examine the basis of Peel's Act. He had made a very close study of English literature on this and allied subjects and had been especially influenced by the writings of James Wilson. It was through Wagner that the chief accusations that

[12] See also his "Essays on Law Reform, Commercial Policy, Banks, etc., in Great Britain and the United States of America," 1859.

[13] "Über die Neuere Entwicklung, etc.," p. 5.

[14] Note that Tellkampf was responsible in co-operation with E. J. Bergius for translating under the title "Geld und Banken" (1859) MacCulloch's "Treatise on Metallic and Paper Money and Banks," in which the currency doctrine is defended.

[15] "Beiträge zur Lehre von den Banken," 1857.

had already been made in England against Peel's Act and the currency doctrine were made available to German readers. His own opinion was that banks should be allowed to set up without legal hindrance, and he opposed the statutory fixing of note issues or of reserve proportions, thus fully supporting the free-banking position. Peel's Act he regarded as being unsound, not only because it was based on the mistaken theories of the currency school, but also on the additional ground that the Bank of England had through its privileged position acquired a responsibility to render aid during a crisis by liberal lending, and now Peel's Act had left its privileges intact but had taken away its obligations.[16] The defect in the system of the great privileged central banks to which he gave most weight was the misuse the Government makes of the power it exercises over such a bank by encouraging it to discount too cheaply and to invest in too much State paper.[17] While the Pereire group in France had assessed the fault of a single privileged central bank to be one of keeping discount rates too high, Wagner held it to be the opposite of keeping lending rates too low.

In the more detailed criticism of the currency doctrine which he published a few years later,[18] prominence was first given in Germany to the theory of *"bankmässige"* cover. This was closely connected up with the celebrated principle of the automatic reflux of notes. The theory was that so long as notes were lent out in true banking business, that is short-term assets, they came back in the natural course of business after the elapse of the loan period and the amount of the issue was supposed for this reason to be constantly subject to check. From this time onwards *"bankmässige"* cover assumed a position of considerable importance in German banking discussions and legislation.

[16] *Op. cit.,* p. 212.
[17] *Op. cit.,* p. 233.
[18] "Die Geld-und Kredittheorie der Peelschen Bankakte," 1862.

The most interesting treatment of the proposals for free banking in Germany is contained in the discussions of the Congress of the *Deutsche Volkswirte*[19] in the early 'sixties and the separate writings of one of its most prominent members, Otto Michaelis. The Congress set out to formulate a legal framework for free banking. It decided that provided unlimited liability were imposed on banking companies, special legal conditions were unnecessary. If limited liability were the rule, however, it might be necessary to formulate certain legal requirements (*Normativbestimmungen*). As to what exactly these conditions should consist of was a matter of some considerable debate, and full agreement was not reached on every point. All the speakers seem to have agreed that no fixed limit should be put on the note issue and that no stipulated reserve proportion should be imposed. They were not quite unanimous on the question whether only certain specified types of assets should be permitted for use as note cover. Max Wirth was of the opinion that all notes should be covered by metal plus *"bankmässige"* bills. He regarded both Government as well as other long-term securities as being too unstable in value to be good note cover.[20] Michaelis thought that neither lombard loans nor State paper were proper cover for notes, and the New York bond deposit system was on this account indefensible. But although he accordingly believed that it was good counsel to recommend to a bank that notes should be covered by *"bankmässige"* bills, he considered that it was not necessary to lay this down as a legislative condition. The Congress was not for the most part in favour of stipulating that bills discounted by

[19] See report of proceedings in the "Vierteljahrschrift für Volkswirtschaft und Kulturgeschichte," 1863, Vol. III., pp. 241 ff.

[20] This discussion in detail of note cover was a new departure in the discussion of banking, and was probably due to two factors peculiar to Germany: firstly, the extreme fluctuations that certainly did take place in the securities of all the German States, including Prussia; and secondly, the fatal experiences in the outlying States of the attempt to use *crédit mobilier* assets as note cover.

a note-issuing bank must have at least two names. Neither did such measures as the placing of restrictions on the amount or type of business other than note issue, legal provisions for the cover of deposits, limitations on the amount of deposit liabilities, or special requirements as to the period of notice for withdrawal of deposits, receive any support. It thus rejected all the Prussian *"Normativbedingungen"* as inappropriate.

The question whether note-holders should be given preferential rights over other creditors (depositors) in the event of a liquidation was answered in the negative. Great importance was attached by all the speakers to the point that the bank should always be obliged to cash notes on the day of presentation on pain of liquidation.[21] This emphasis on the necessity for the rigid enforcement of the liquidation penalty for a failure to meet obligations was something of a departure from what had been customary in the past. Observations had from time to time been made on the need for the enforcement of quick resumptions of payments, for the imposition of penalties varying with the length of time for which the suspension lasted, and for liquidation after a

[21] Michaelis says: "Das einzige reelle Sicherungsmittel ist das bei der Bank stets wache Gefühl der Notengefahr. Man sage daher, so viel Noten als einer Bank jeden Tag zur Einlösung präsentiert werden, so viel muss sie *an dem Tag der Präsentierung* unter allen Umständen einlösen, und wenn sie das nicht tut, *so ist sie bankrott.*" See "Vierteljahrschrift für Volkswirtschaft und Kulturgeschichte," 1863, Vol. III., p. 251. It is important that it should be clear that this does not mean that a bank would never be able to tide over a temporary embarrassment, or, alternatively, that it would be compelled, in order to be perfectly secure, to keep reserves of 100 percent. It is, indeed, to be expected that the volume of notes flowing back to any bank will, from time to time, surpass the normal anticipated movement plus a certain allowance for some margin of deviation for which the bank can be expected to provide adequate reserves. But if such a surprise demand for cash suddenly arises and the bank's position is such as to allow it to meet all its obligations, provided it had the time to call in loans and so liquidate its position, it will surely be able to borrow for the necessary period from the market. A bank which is solvent to the extent that it could meet its liabilities within a reasonably short period, but was suffering from insufficient liquidity at the moment, should not experience difficulties in arranging such a loan.

more or less lengthy period, but it was usually taken for granted that a suspension for a certain length of time was permissible and normal.

Particular emphasis was placed by Michaelis, and the Congress as a whole, on the, up till now, neglected importance of deposit banking, and the Congress resolved that the setting up of discount and deposit banks should be recommended,[22] and when it again approached the subject two years later,[23] Michaelis was very much in favour of making the campaign for the development of banking independent of the fight for freedom in note-issuing, because he recognised how remote were the chances of success of the latter. This was in spite of his being in sharp disagreement so far as the theory of the subject was concerned with the common view that notes and deposits were to be rigidly contrasted.

In an article published in 1865,[24] Michaelis argued that by establishing unity in the note issue, one of the most important checks on over-expansion was removed. With a large number of banks the average period of circulation of notes was shortened; each note had more chance of coming back to the issuer for cash payment. Now in the case of deposit credits, he says, the limits to expansion are even narrower. The test of cashability comes very early; a check is not likely to change hands many times by endorsement and will often be paid in immediately to his bank by the person in whose favour it is drawn. Every check drawn in favour of someone outside the circle of customers of that bank on which it is drawn will be paid in at another bank, thus giving the latter a claim on the former, and unless it is balanced by a counter-claim, the one will lose cash to the other. While admitting to

---

[22] *Op. cit.*, p. 258.

[23] See "Vierteljahrschrift für Volkswirtschaft und Kulturgeschichte," 1865, Vol. II., pp. 206 ff.

[24] "Noten und Depositen," published in Faucher's "Vierteljahrschrift."

this extent a certain difference between checks and notes (the latter were likely to remain for a longer average period in circulation outside the banks before being paid in), and this was the only distinction of any importance that had yet been recognised, Michaelis did not see in it sufficient reason for withholding freedom from the note-issuing business while allowing it to deposit banking. In both cases, so long as there were a number of banks, a strict control would be exercised by and among the banks themselves. In both cases monopoly increased the circulation period and deferred the test of cashability.

Michaelis was convinced that there exists in a multiple banking system an automatic mechanism which checks any tendencies to expansion of the note issue. And this, he said, will work so long as there are some or even one of the banks that does not expand.[25] He thus regards it not only as a means of checking any single bank getting out of step with the rest, but as a mechanism which, since not all banks without *any* exception are likely to set the process of expansion going at the same time, will keep the whole system under control. Longfield's objection would, if it is valid, apply *a fortiori* to this case, but it remained more or less unknown.

To those who argued in favour of unity because it widened the area over which the notes of any bank could be used, Michaelis replied that it was a positive advantage from the point of view of limiting the note issue if the territorial

---

[25] "Nehmen wir an, das alle nebeneinander bestehenden Banken gleich leichtsinnig in der Ausdehnung ihres Notenumlauf wären, so würde durch solche gegenseitige Abrechnung im Ganzen eine Kompensation, nicht eine Realisation der Notenversprechungen stattfinden. Da indess die verschiedenen Banken verschiedenen Grundsätze verfahren, so führt diese Abrechnung zur Notwendigkeit barer Ausgleichungen sobald nur eine unter ihnen ist, die im Verhältniss zu ihren Umsätzen wenig Noten im Umlauf hat. Denn diese eine empfängt immer mehr fremde Noten als andere Banken von den ihrigen empfangen haben können. . . . " Article "Noten und Depositen," pp. 130–131, in Faucher's "Vierteljahrschrift," 1865; also republished by Michaelis in his "Volkswirtschaftliche Schriften," Vol. II., 1873.

area of circulation of the notes of any bank were small, since it made their return to the issuer more frequent.[26]

It was at about this time that the first publication[27] appeared of a writer who has, perhaps, received far less attention than his work merited. We refer to Philip Joseph Geyer. He was, in common with Tellkampf, an adherent of the stricter form of the currency theory. He started off from the thesis that the amount of money in circulation should always remain constant,[28] and that the movement away from an approximation to such a state of affairs had been caused by the issue of bank notes not covered by specie. He held that only fully-covered note issues are a "real" economic factor, uncovered note issues merely bring "artificial" capital (*künstliches Kapital*) into operation, and if more artificial capital comes forward than there is real (*natürliches*) capital lying idle, a crisis results from the phenomenon of overproduction.[29] While being violently opposed to freedom of note issue, he was very much in favour of giving freedom to set up deposit banks which would collect and use the idle real savings. He speaks of such a process making the uncovered note issue unnecessary.

After the crisis of 1857 and the operations as lender of last resort then carried out by the Bank of England, there had

---

[26] "Je grösser der territoriale Umlaufsbezirk der Noten einer Bank, um so leichter sammelm sich also Notenmassen im Verkehr an, auf deren Rückkehr die Bank nicht vorbereitet ist, je kleiner derselbe, um so öfter kommen die Noten in den Fall, gegen Bar umgewechselt werden zu müssen, weil sie um so öfter in Hände kommen die Zahlungen aus dem Umlaufsbezirk heraus zu machen haben"—Article above quoted, p. 132. Actually the principle of limiting the area served by one bank would lead to conditions of monopoly rather than of competition. The more natural system would be a branch system in which the area over which the notes of any bank circulate is wide and in which branches of different banks compete in the same district. If Michaelis' other check—namely, the clearing mechanism which he supposed to function between banks in the same district—works, then inter-bank control will not be lacking in effectiveness in such a system.

[27] "Banken und Krisen," 1865.

[28] *Op. cit.*, p. 7.

[29] *Op. cit.*, pp. 33 ff.

been noticeable even in Germany something of a change of emphasis in the arguments for central banking. The advocates of a strong central bank ceased to support it merely because they thought it was the only way of keeping note issues within the necessary bounds and increased the emphasis on panic financiering. This attitude was clearly stated by Professor Nasse in a pamphlet he published early in 1866.[30] Whereas small note issuers were always discredited during a crisis, the notes of a central bank could continue to satisfy the internal currency demands. Therefore, by avoiding the necessity of providing for an internal drain of metal on top of the external drain, central banking rendered the crisis less serious. For these reasons Nasse welcomed the idea of the Prussian Bank becoming a central bank and opposed Peel's Act, which takes from such a bank the possibility of filling up the gaps made in the credit system of a country by a crisis. His attack on the principle of Peel's Act was directed against a Bill just introduced into the Prussian legislature by Michaelis for the fixing of the fiduciary issue of the Prussian Bank.

It would at first sight seem a little strange that such a Bill should be sponsored by Michaelis, who had always been in favour of the fullest freedom for note-issuing banks and a minimum of legislative interference. His attitude is, however, perfectly consistent with his general thesis. Where there are a large number of banks, there is an automatic check on the note issue; in the case of a privileged monopoly this mechanism is absent and therefore some external limit must be imposed.[31]

Nasse agreed with Michaelis that note cover should as far as possible be kept *"bankmässige"* (short-term commit-

[30] "Die Preussische Bank und die Ausdehnung ihres Geschäftskreises in Deutschland," 1866.
[31] "Volkswirtschaftliche Schriften," Vol. II., p. 383; the relevant passage was absent from the article ("Noten und Depositen") as published in Faucher's "Vierteljahrschrift."

ments). This excluded Government securities and was in direct opposition to the basis of Peel's Act, under which the fiduciary issue could be backed only by Government securities.[32]

Geyer and Tellkampf both elaborated their views further in 1867.[33] Geyer summarises the faults of the present banking system under two heads: first, that it provides the material for trade crises and production cycles by producing "artificial capital" up to a point where there is an excessive amount of capital in existence, and, secondly, that having produced the crisis, it intensifies it by contracting credit and causing forced sales. His explanation of the original of the boom came very close to the modern "over-investment" theories of the Austrian school, but he failed to give any acceptable explanation of the more immediate cause of the crisis and depression. His reasoning here develops into an under-consumption theory. The over-supply of capital results in the over-production of consumption goods, which he believes cannot be absorbed by the market, because the demand for consumption goods will only increase with a fall in their price, and while it is true that cheaper capital reduces interest charges, this is so small an item as to be hardly perceptible in the final price of goods ready for consumption.

He approaches the theory of banking somewhat along the lines of the modern theory of the equation between investment and real savings. The difficulties which accompany the solution of the bank question lie not so much in the theory, he says, as in the practice.[34] The theory is clear, that the uncovered note issue should be brought into equilibrium

---

[32] The reason, as Nasse explains, was that Prussian Government securities were far less stable than English ones, and in case of need could often only be realised at a considerable loss. He even suggested that it might be advisable for the Prussian Bank to invest its spare funds in English Treasury Bills.

[33] P. J. Geyer, "Theorie und Praxis des Zettelbankwesens nebst einer Charakteristik der Englischen, Französischen und Preussischen Bank," 1867; J. L. Tellkampf, "Die Prinzipien des Geld-und Bankwesens," 1867.

[34] *Op. cit.*, p. 227.

with the amount of capital lying idle, but as we do not know the amount of this idle capital, it is impossible to effect an equilibrium. He concluded that it is advisable to give up altogether the issue of uncovered notes and that the idle capital could better be collected by extending deposit banking. In the period of change-over, the reduction of artificial bank money should follow in step with the increase in deposits, and to accomplish this it is necessary that the note issue should be centralised and confined to a single institution. He realised that even given this unity in the note issue there would still be international complications; it would be pointless as well as difficult for any one country in isolation to give up "artificial bank capital," since it would be affected by the creation of bank capital in other countries and would probably be unable to hold out against the lower discount rates elsewhere.

Peel's Act was not a commendable solution to Geyer's problem because it did not carry the currency principle to its logical conclusion. It should either forbid uncovered notes altogether or else arrange that they should be equal to the idle money capital. Since it did neither of these things it could not prevent crises, and once crises arose, it led to further complications by provoking panics instead of easing credit conditions so as to reduce trade losses.

The attitude taken up by both Geyer and Tellkampf in demanding the total abolition of the fiduciary issue ignored several important aspects of the monetary problem. Starting, as they do, from a situation where the existing money supply already contains notes in large proportion not covered 100 percent by metal, they underestimate the difficulties of the deflationary process which would be involved in getting back to their "ideal" situation, and which would entail a much more violent and lasting disturbance than any which was likely to occur from the movement they fear in the opposite direction. And, what is more important, perhaps, the objective would have no real value, since there is no special sanctity of any specific figure for the total quantity of money. All that is important are fluctuations in this total quantity, and all that Geyer's theory required was that no *further* increases should take place, so that the economic system, once having got into equilibrium with the amount of money in existence at the moment, will not be required to readjust repeatedly in the future.

In confining their considerations to bank-notes and the effect of these on the total quantity of money, they ignore also complications introduced by the existence of demand deposits and the effects of changes in their velocity. We start from a position where we have a volume of demand deposits which have arisen, not (or not all) from payments into the banks of an equivalent amount of cash, but from the redeposit of loans (also not backed 100 percent by cash) made previously by the banks, and these demand deposits alter the volume of effective circulating media of exchange by changes in their velocity of circulation (number of checks drawn per period of time).

The criterion of keeping the amount of the circulation constant may at times, then, positively require the amount of currency in the form of bank-notes to increase. Such would, for instance, be the case where a decline in the activity of deposits (increase in the average period for which they remain idle) requires the banks to make fresh loans if they are to keep the effective circulation the same as it was before, and the new borrowers prefer bank-notes to demand deposits. Once the deposits have been created, it is immaterial so far as the economic results are concerned what part of them is changed into currency, and the only deciding factor would seem to be the choice of the public as to which they prefer, deposits on current account or bank-notes.

The less extreme currency school writers, as well as the banking school, regarded notes as rendering a service in what they called "economising specie," which is usually to be interpreted as "providing easier credit." Geyer and Tellkampf, adherents of the very strictest currency doctrine, look upon them only as a more convenient form in which money can be carried about or transported. It is noticeable also that where people like Tooke and Wagner saw as the sole evil of increasing the amount of currency the possibility that it might depreciate its value (raise the price level), and therefore concluded, that since an increase in its volume had frequently taken place without causing a decrease in its purchasing power, it was not always an evil,[35] Geyer did at least see that changes in the quantity of circulating media produced changes in the structure of production with certain undesirable repercussions.

In his later work Tellkampf still considered that if the plan of unifying the note issue and restricting it to the amount of specie deposited could not be put into operation, then the next best alternative was the Scotch system, and he seems to have regarded this as a very good second best.

The discussions conclude in Germany with a few publications at the beginning of the 'seventies, just prior to the foundation of the Reichsbank. Among these was a pamphlet by Leopold Lasker,[36] who alleged, probably not unjustifiably,[37] that it had still not been conclusively shown why banking should be made the exception from the rule of private enterprise in all branches of economic life, and that no case had yet been made out against "*Bankfreiheit.*" Two treatises on banking and credit were also published in these years by Wagner and Knies[38] respectively. These two were support-

---

[35] See Wagner, "Beiträge zur Lehre von den Banken," pp. 81–86.

[36] "Bankfreiheit oder nicht?" 1871.

[37] Especially as Longfield's argument remained practically unknown.

[38] A. Wagner, "System der deutschen Zettelbankgesetzgebung unter Vergleichung mit der Ausländischen, zugleich ein Handbuch des Zettelbankwesens," 1870–73. C. G. A. Knies, "Geld und Kredit" (two volumes), 1873–79.

ers of opposite sides in the controversy, but Wagner had by now obviously come under the influence of the historical school and therefore was no longer so uncompromisingly in favour of the free-banking system, and insisted that there could be no absolute solution in favour of one system; all systems can be justified in the appropriate circumstances. He had, however, abandoned few of the essentials of his old position, and the bias is still towards the free-banking ideal.

One of the theories he sought to destroy was the idea that note-issuing brought in a fabulous profit. This idea was one of the grounds of objection to free banking held by Knies, who wrote that the creation of bank-notes must be subject to special regulations,[39] because their creation was costless. Wagner pointed out the existence of costs of management, and especially the costs of the substantial capital that was necessary for a note-issuing business.

Neither did Wagner admit that it was necessary to single out banking from among all other branches of industrial activity and subject it to unlimited liability provisions. But he allowed that it might be an advantage to reform the whole of the company law so as to enforce special requirements for different types of undertaking, and with this idea in mind he set out to formulate the *"Normativbedingungen"* that might be applied to the case of banking. Accordingly, he suggested that the bank's capital should be required to attain a certain figure, that there should be a limit on the lowest denomination for notes, that there should be a regular exchange of notes once or twice a week between banks, and that the principle of publicity should be enforced. Such regulations as these he regarded as being perfectly compatible with the idea of full *"Bankfreiheit."* Other clauses frequently to be found in bank laws, such as regulated the business of the banks, fixed the relation between the amount of the note

[39] *Op. cit.*, Vol. I., p. 313.

issue and the amount of the bank's capital or determined the form of the note cover, were not compatible with full *"Bankfreiheit,"* but if complete *"Bankfreiheit"* was looked upon with suspicion, some clauses of this kind might be conceded.

In common with Michaelis, he placed emphasis on the necessity for a speedy liquidation of insolvent banks. If a note when presented for redemption is not paid at the bank's chief place of business or at its redemption counters and branches, and within a short period—three days is the time he suggests—the bank can still not pay its obligations, any creditor of the bank should be allowed to bring a demand before the courts for its liquidation. The only extenuating circumstances should be cases of *forces majeures,* such as a foreign invasion.[40]

Wagner took sides against Michaelis on the question of whether, once it was decided to impose reserve requirements for the note issue, it was better to use the Continental or German method (*"Dritteldeckung,"* or one-third specie cover) or the Peel system (fixed fiduciary issue). Knies and Michaelis both favoured the Peel system. Wagner preferred the *"Dritteldeckung,"* because, although it was true that the figure of one-third was purely arbitrary, it is far less rigid than the Peel system or the American bond deposit system.

Commenting on the 1866 experiences in Germany, which had turned the thoughts of many people towards a consideration and affirmation of the advantages of a central bank, Wagner agrees that it had evidenced advantages. He submits, however, that they were not necessarily such as could only be gained by privileged or entirely monopolistic central banks, and that not only the Prussian Bank but also similar great banks in important cities such as the Frankfurt, Leipzig and Bremen banks, smaller central banks or central banks of

[40] *Op. cit.,* p. 634.

second order as they might be called, had given support to reputable firms at the height of the crisis.[41]

The partial recantation of Wagner, the once relentless champion of *Bankfreiheit,* may be fairly regarded as the end of the active opposition to central banking in Germany.

---

[41] *Op. cit.,* p. 357.

CHAPTER X

The Post-1848
Discussions
in England

The account we have so far given of the development of English thought on the merits and demerits of a free-banking system, as compared with one in which the note issue was monopolised, brought us up to James Wilson's contribution at the close of the 'forties. In England, at least after 1844, if not before, the only practical problem was always whether, *given central banking*, there should be limitations or no limitations on the amount of the note circulation. The question of whether there should be freedom or privilege in the issue of notes was scarcely ever raised. But the discussion of its latter problem on a much more extensive scale by the economists and financial experts on the Continent could not fail entirely to draw the attention of their English contemporaries.

The economic literature of the 'fifties in England showed an almost complete neglect of this problem: there were not many more than a couple of references to it. Of these one was due to R. H. Mills, professor in one of the Irish Universities, who treated the subject in the course of a series of lectures which were later published.[1] In his view, "a violent expansion and contraction of the currency . . . is the inevita-

---

[1] "The Principles of Currency and Banking," 1857.

ble result of a system which has still many advocates and which has but late been checked . . . that of allowing a number of banks of issue to subsist in the country."[2] In support of this statement he quotes verbatim the argument given by Longfield, and this citation appears to be right up to the present day[3] the only instance of any mention of Longfield's point, in spite of its being the most important single controversial point in the theory of the problem.

The other reference to which we have referred came from the pen of Herbert Spencer,[4] and is a denunciation of all State interference in banking and a plea for the strict application of the laws of bankruptcy to banks which suspend cash payments. He believed that this would be a sufficient and effective check against over-issues.

In the 'sixties several circumstances combined to bring the controversy again into the open. The currency disorders in the United States of America, and the publication of Coullet's book, "La Circulation Monétaire," in France in 1865, invited comments in *The Economist*. This journal, following in the tradition of Wilson, under the editorship of his son-in-law, Walter Bagehot, continued to make frequent reference to the superior qualities of a plural banking system. The evidence given before the French Banking Commission and the not very encouraging first experiences of the new National Banking system in America provided the occasion for further remarks to the same effect from time to time in 1867.

The French influence was particularly strong. Bonamy Price, Professor of Political Economy at Oxford, drew attention to the points of disagreement between the leading pro-

---

[2] *Op. cit.*, p. 70.

[3] Neisser has recently used the same argument in his article "Notenbankfreiheit?" in the *Weltwirtschaftliches Archiv.*, October, 1930.

[4] "Essays on State Tampering with Money and Banks," first published in the *Westminster Review*, 1858, and later included in Vol. III. of "Essays Scientific, Political and Speculative."

tagonists, Wolowski and Chevalier.[5] In addition, direct connections were established between the English and French economists via the *Enquête*. Bagehot was called to give evidence before the Commission in person, and written memoranda were submitted by Hankey, Newmarch, Patterson and J. S. Mill. Wolowski visited London in 1866 and attended the meeting of the Political Economy Club, where Bagehot was reading a paper on whether it was better "to entrust the principal custody of the bullion reserves against banking liabilities to a single bank or to distribute it between several banks."[6]

The English reaction to the adoption by the Bank of France of the policy of moving the rate of discount in response to changes in its reserve position was, in general, one of approval. It was hailed by *The Economist* as the recognition at long last of a principle which this journal had been advocating in its pages for many years. The theory of discount rate, though as yet imperfectly understood as to the details of all its effects, and especially of its effects on the price and income structure of the country concerned, had received fairly general acceptance in England under the influence of the writings of MacLeod[7] and Goschen,[8] who had at least made it clear to the banking world that the discount rate could be used to influence the balance of payments and gold flows.

Goschen made a direct attack on the low discount rate school in France,[9] and insisted that the higher rate of discount which had prevailed over the preceding few years must be interpreted as the result, not of the artificial tampering with the natural state of things as Pereires claimed, but

[5] See *Fraser's Magazine*, 1868, "The Controversy on Free Banking between M. Wolowski and M. Michel Chevalier." Bonamy Price's own treatment of the problem contributed nothing very new. See his "Principles of Currency," 1869.

[6] See "Political Economy Club, Centenary Volume," Vol. VI., p. 86.

[7] "Theory and Practice of Banking," 1855.

[8] "Foreign Exchanges," 1861.

[9] Article entitled "Seven Per Cent." in the *Edinburgh Review*, January, 1865; republished in his "Essays and Addresses on Economic Questions."

as the result of the free play of natural forces which had raised the demand for free capital and therefore its price.

Nevertheless, the views of the Pereire group in France were not without protagonists in England. Best known among them was a journalist named Patterson, who gained sufficient recognition to be invited to submit a memorandum to the French Commission.[10] He extended to the case of the Bank of England the view that it was the monopoly of the note issue and the monopolist's attempt to maximise profits which caused it to raise the rate of interest. Changes in the rate of discount were an unmixed evil to be avoided at all costs except in so far as under a free and competitive system of note issue they would become "natural."[11] The monopoly of the Bank of England was attacked also by Guthrie.[12] Although in many respects a crank, he called attention to one important aspect of a free-banking multiple reserve system. He submitted that under free banking, where each bank would be obliged to hold its own gold reserves, there would be a much closer connection between note issues and gold reserves, and that over-issues and the drains of bullion to which they led could be checked before they became dangerous. Should the tendency show itself, he said, "All the banks, being at the same time dealers in bullion and in discounts *and holding only the quantity of bullion required as the basis of their own trade,* would at once feel the withdrawal of gold from their coffers and be *all constrained immediately without reference either to their issues or deposits* to reduce the amount of their discounts in proportion to the cash they hold."[13] This would mean that in a free-banking system banks could not escape from a strict adherence to the rules of the gold standard and the currency

[10] See "Evidence," Vol. V., p. 559.
[11] "The Economy of Capital," 1864.
[12] "Bank Monopoly, The Cause of Commercial Crises," 1864.
[13] *Op. cit.,* p. 41.

principle, but the whole tenour of these remarks was in curious contradiction to a thesis of the same author's, that it was a mistaken policy for the Bank of England to keep a fixed price for gold instead of allowing its price to vary just like that of any ordinary commodity in response to changes in supply and demand. The monopoly of the Bank of England was, according to Guthrie, the primary cause of commercial crises. MacLeod also stated this view but did not effectively substantiate it.[14]

Another feature of Continental thought at this time which had its counterpart in England was the attack on all fiduciary issues, led by Cernuschi and Modeste in France, and Tellkampf and Geyer in Germany. The English sponsor of these doctrines was Edmund Philipps.[15] He was chronologically prior to the Continental exponents except for Tellkampf, but attracted much less attention. He believed that so long as the Bank of England issued more notes than it had gold to redeem, it would be forced on occasions to suddenly call in its notes and raise discount rates, and he went so far as to suggest that if the Bank of England would not accept a charter under the condition that convertibility in his sense should be maintained, any of the joint stock banks would be pleased to do so.[16] This kind of argument never gained any following in England, however, and passed practically unnoticed.

Let us now revert to the more general aspects of the question of unity as against plurality in the note issue. Bagehot's remarks before the French Commission were confined to the specific questions relating to the French case. The French system was inferior to the English system, he said, because in England each little town had its two or three

---

[14] See his "Theory and Practice of Banking," Vol. I (p. 479 in the 1902 edition).
[15] "A Plea for the Reform of the British Currency and the Bank of England Charter," 1861.
[16] *Op. cit.*, p. 11.

banks and these provided facilities for the collection and utilisation of savings such as did not exist in France. On being asked whether unity or plurality in the banking system would be the best system for England, he replied that the question was at the moment indifferent to her, because the result that the multiplicity of banks serves to obtain had already been reached: the collection of idle savings and the prevention of "their going to waste" was already well accomplished. On the theoretical question, he added, he was not required to speak.[17]

It was the opinion of J. S. Mill, as expressed in his written memorandum to the *Enquête*, that the importance of the choice between unity and plurality of banks had been exaggerated. It had been generally assumed that a plural banking system would increase credit facilities, and this assumption had been the reason both for the praise of the partisans and for the opposition of the enemies of a plural system. But Mill thought that, in fact, the system would realise neither the benefits claimed by the one side nor the inconveniences envisaged by the other, because after a period of adjustment, we should, he believed, find the note circulation distributed among a certain number of banks who would collectively conduct themselves in much the same way and provide just about the same credit facilities as the single bank under the old system. No one bank could augment its issues except momentarily, because of losing its reserves to other banks, and an increase in credit would take place only when it was provoked or favoured by general causes acting on all banks at once, and every time such causes came into play they exerted an exactly similar influence on the single bank in a unitary system. There would consequently be no very great practical difference between the two systems.[18]

[17] "Evidence," Vol. I., p. 35.

[18] See "Evidence," Vol. V., pp. 592–3. See also his evidence before the English Select Committee on the Bank Acts, 1857, Q. 2039.

That Bagehot, on the other hand, thought that there would be very real and important differences between the two systems became clear in his writings in *The Economist* and in his book "Lombard Street," which he published in 1873. In the first place, it was the advantage of the multiple system of local issues that it produced a much more rapid development of banking over the country. A diffused system of note issue prepares the way for deposit business by establishing the credit of the banker. It is much easier to establish this by way of note issue, because the initiative is more on the side of the banker than in pure deposit banking. Moreover, such a system was better adjusted to loan business, because the partners in provincial banks usually belong to the district and have local knowledge which puts them in a better position to estimate the risks involved in lending to particular enterprise of individuals. Whatever had been the faults of the country note-issuing bankers, and acknowledging that we might not wish to see their return, they had done us a great service in the beginning. It was because we in this country had had a diffused system of note issue in the early days that we had outstripped other countries in all types of banking business. Admittedly, after a country has once succeeded in developing a paper currency and the other banking business to which this is an introduction—by whatever means this has been accomplished and however slowly or rapidly—the case for a multiple system of note issue ceases to be of so much practical importance, and Bagehot always refers to the question as being one of deciding whether it is advisable, *in the abstract, and when we begin de novo* to grant a monopoly. Accordingly, there was in his view no case for the Pereire plan of setting up a second bank of about equal strength alongside the Bank of France, in Paris, because Paris had already become accustomed to a note circulation, and in any case he thought the plan deserving of grave suspicion, since it came from the same people who objected to a rise in the discount rate. So far as provincial banking was concerned, it was plain that facilities were poorly developed as compared with England and Scotland, and this must be attributed to the lack of country issues in France. Nevertheless, he did not feel justified in advocating a return to a system similar to the old departmental banking system, because, he remarks rather cynically, "we may lay down a principle that every credit currency permitted in France should be such as *could be made legal tender the day after a revolution.*"[19] Considering the problem quite apart from such questions of expediency, however, he was convinced that a country starting *de novo* would do better to have a multiple reserve system, such as that of New York, rather than the English or French system[20] of a privileged monopoly which was essentially a single reserve system. It was not yet generally understood that the Banking Department of the Bank of England did in fact hold the only reserve of ready cash against the banking liabilities of the country, and it was important to make clear the effects of this on the position of the Bank. We had in England evolved a system in which not only practically the whole of the gold reserve (*i.e.*, the reserve against notes), but also the whole of the banking reserve (*i.e.*, the reserve against deposits) of the country was kept by a single institution. This had grown out of the privileged position in which that institution, the Bank of England, had been placed by Government interference in banking. "The natural system—that which would have sprung up if the Government had left banking alone—is that of many banks of equal or not altogether unequal size."[21] Instead of that, we had a central bank, and a central banking system had certain characteristics, liable to become danger-

---

[19] See *The Economist*, February 11th, 1865, p. 158.

[20] In Germany the Prussian Bank was not yet a bankers' bank holding the bulk of the cash of the other banks, and therefore differed in this respect from the Banks of England and France. See Nasse, "Die Preussische Bank, etc.," p. 59.

[21] "Lombard Street," p. 66.

ous if not very carefully handled, which distinguished it from decentralised multiple reserve system. The two respects in which the centralised system showed the most marked difference were, firstly, in the effect on the total cash reserves of the banking system as a whole, and secondly, the reliance on a "lender of last resort."

The commercial banks under this system, instead of keeping each its own gold reserves, keep their reserves in Bank of England notes or in claims, in the form of deposits at the Bank, on Bank of England notes. Each bank in estimating the proper distribution of its assets between immediately realisable and less immediately realisable, so as to ensure what it thinks is the necessary degree of liquidity, regards what it holds on deposit at the Bank of England as "as good as cash," so that according to the calculations of the commercial banks their cash reserves should amount, in addition to the sums of actual cash they keep in their tills, to the whole of that sum which appears on the Bank of England's books as bankers' deposits. But what the Bank of England has at any time available in cash, that is, notes in the Banking Department, is always very much less than this—it is only half or even a third of its deposit liabilities—because the Bank relends part of the reserves of the commercial banks. The virtual pooling of the reserves of all the separate banks means that in normal times the Bank of England can count on withdrawals by one bank being counterbalanced by additional depositing by others. The difficulty arises in times of pressure all round, when all banks are likely to be requiring cash at the same time, and it is then that the disadvantages of the single reserve system become apparent. The actual reserve held by the Bank is smaller than the sum of the amounts calculated by all the separate banks to ensure safety and which would really exist in reserve under a decentralised system. The spare cash of the money market is thus reduced to a smaller amount than under the alternative multiple reserve system. MacCulloch had supposed that banking reserves would be larger under a unitary than under a plural system; Bagehot showed that they were smaller.

The second weakness of a central banking system is its tendency to create points in the system at which distress support is given. The existence of such refuges becomes part of the data on which the banks base their policy. It destroys some responsibilities and creates others. It is bound to happen that a central banking system being created by State aid is more likely than a natural system to require State help, and what it knows it can depend on, it will not hesitate to utilise. This circumstance in turn leads the public to demand extra services from the central bank in times of extremity and expects that it should help the smaller establishments, and "it is," says Bagehot, "a serious difficulty that the same bank which keeps the ultimate reserve should also have the duty of lending in the last resort. The two functions are, in practice, inconsistent—one prescribes keeping money and the other prescribes parting with money."[22]

It is this part of the central bank's activities—acting as "lender of last resort"—that has been singled out by Hawtrey[23] as constituting the primary function of a central bank. In what Bagehot called "the natural system," no bank would have any special claim on any other.

In spite of the, in his opinion, manifested disadvantages of a central banking system, Bagehot saw no chance of giving it up and going over to a many reserve system: such an idea he admitted was childish, because it would take decades to build up another system of credit to replace the trust that had now come to be placed in the Bank of England as the pivot of the whole structure. Instead, therefore, of advocating the adoption of the alternative system, he tried only to

[22] See *The Economist,* September 1st, 1866.
[23] See "The Art of Central Banking," Chapter IV.

elucidate canons of policy which would facilitate the less imperfect working of the one we now had.

It had been Bagehot's aim to make the Bank Directors realise the *double strain* placed on the Bank's cash resources in times of stress by the dual nature of its position, on the one side as holder of the banker's reserves, and on the other as lender of last resort. Firstly, it must be prepared to provide cash to the banks in respect of what was in all respects their own (viz., Bank of England deposits held as reserve), and secondly, it must provide cash by way of loan to help such institutions as find their own cash resources insufficient.[24] This led him up to his final conclusion that the Bank must adopt a more cautious policy and that a banking reserve of one-third in normal times was too low.

Bagehot's influence on the shaping of central bank policy must have been more considerable than that of any other single writer either here or on the Continent. It was mainly as a result of his continued emphasis that it came to be commonly admitted that the correct policy for the central bank in the crisis was to lend freely at a high rate of interest. He did a great deal to secure the recognition of the nature of the special responsibilities of a central bank. His accepted thesis was a rebuttal of what was considered at the time to be one of the cardinal principles of the 1844 Act, namely, that the Bank of England should be released from any obligation to pay attention to the public interest in framing its policy and should be at liberty to act for the benefit of its shareholders, the principles of management by the Banking Department being the same as those regulating any other large deposit bank. J. S. Mill had supposed this principle to have been already rejected by 1857.[25] But it was not easy to obtain general agreement among the

---

[24] The fact that in England the Bank does not lend directly to the banks (by rediscounting) but to the bill brokers is immaterial. It provides the bill brokers with the wherewithal to make repayments to the banks.

[25] See the Select Committee on the Bank Acts, 1857, Q. 2032.

Bank Directors. Immediately after the crisis of 1866 the Governor of the Bank made a public announcement before the proprietors that the Bank had conceived a duty to have been imposed on it of supporting the banking community and had accordingly lent unflinchingly during the crisis at a cost of a great reduction in its reserves.[26] Bagehot took this as an acknowledgment by the Bank that it kept not merely the currency reserve (gold) of the country, but also the banking reserve, and that it should use the funds of which it was thus given command to help the banking community in time of a crisis.[27] One of the Bank Directors and a former Governor, Thomson Hankey, denied vehemently that any such responsibility had been admitted.[28] He regarded it as a most pernicious doctrine to expect the Bank to do what was quite inconsistent with the ordinary workings of a deposit bank, namely, to make advances when the public demanded them to an almost unlimited extent, and maintained that the banking community must be taught not to rely on the Bank coming to their aid when they had rendered their own assets unavailable. In these circumstances a banking reserve of one-third against deposits was ample. Hankey's views were defended also by G. W. Norman.[29]

Bagehot replied that whether the Bank Directors approved in principle or not, the Bank had, in fact, established a guiding precedent by lending freely in previous panics (as in both 1857 and 1866), and such action had become the legitimate expectation of the money market. If the Bank Directorate wanted to repudiate this obligation, it should make an official and unequivocal announcement to that effect.[30]

Bagehot's "Lombard Street" really concluded controver-

[26] They fell from £5,800,000 to £1,200,000 in a week.
[27] See *The Economist*, September 22nd, 1866.
[28] See his "Principles of Banking, Its Utility and Economy; with Remarks on the Working and Management of the Bank of England" (2nd Edition, 1867), pp. 1–39.
[29] See *The Economist*, December 22nd, 1866, p. 1488.
[30] *Ibid.*, December 8th, pp. 1418–9.

sial discussion on the relative merits of free banking and central banking. Its theme was that we find ourselves in possession of an anomalous banking system. It is not the most perfect if we were able to choose from the beginning, but now that we have it we must make the best of it by clearly recognising its weaknesses, accepting the responsibilities it creates, and keeping adequate funds on hand to meet them.

We find Goschen re-echoing Bagehot's warnings respecting the inadequateness of reserves about twenty years later in connection with the Baring crisis of 1890.[31]

*   *   *

We show below the chief disputants in the free-banking controversy cross-grouped with their standpoint towards the banking and currency controversy:

	Free	*Central*
	Parnell	Tooke
	Wilson	Bonamy Price
	MacLeod	Cairnes[32]
	Courcelle-Seneuil	Coullet
	Coquelin	
	Chevalier	
Banking School	Coq	
	Garnier	
	Mannequin	
	Brasseur	
	Horn	
	Wagner	
	Lasker	

[31] "Essays and Addresses on Economic Questions," 1891. Essay entitled "Our Cash Reserves and Central Stock of Gold."

[32] See his pamphlet (1854), "An Examination into the Principles of Currency involved in the Bank Charter Act of 1844," pp. 62 ff.

		MacCulloch
		G. W. Norman
		Loyd
		Longfield
		R. H. Mills
Currency School	Cernuschi	Lavergne
		d'Eichtal
		Wolowski
	Hübner	Tellkampf
	Michaelis	Geyer
		Knies
	Mises	Neisser

CHAPTER XI

Discussions in America Prior to the Foundation of the Federal Reserve System

After 1875 the central banking systems of those countries which already had them were accepted without further discussion, and the practical choice of the one system in preference to the alternative was never again questioned. Moreover, the declared superiority of central banking became nothing less than a dogma without any very clear understanding of the exact nature of the advantages, but there remained one among the chief commercial countries of the world which still lacked a central banking organisation: this was the United States of America. It is the purpose of this chapter to examine some of the motives which led to the final adoption of such an organisation by that country in 1913.

As we have previously described, the banking structure of the United States consisted of a multitude of small independent banks, each with its business confined to a narrow area. There were in 1913 over 20,000 banks, of which about 7,000 were National Banks issuing notes and the rest non-note-issuing banks operating, not under the National Bank Law, but under the banking law of the States in which they lay.

This was frequently cited as an example of the practical application of the principles of free banking. But while it was true that any person or group of persons complying with certain requirements could open a bank of issue, and that the business was open to all on the same terms, there were at least two important points of divergence between the American "free banking" so called and free banking in the more general sense in which the term was used by the writers on the continent of Europe. Firstly, the banks were excluded from practically all possibilities of developing branch organisation, and most banks outside the big cities approached more or less to local monopolies. Secondly, the National Banking Law, under which the "free" banks operated, specified a peculiar system of note issue. It is at least a supportable view that the American bank organisation lacked the advantages of both central banking and of free banking proper.

Practically all tendencies to the growth of branch banking which had manifested themselves as part of the natural evolution of banking development elsewhere had been expressly excluded in the United States. In the days before the National Banking Law, banks had come exclusively under the jurisdiction of the individual States, and banking firms authorised to set up in one State had no possibility of extending their operations by branch office or otherwise beyond the boundaries of this State into the territory of another. So far as the allowance of branch banking within the confines of the individual State was concerned, the practice varied. Some States, mostly in the south, had permitted it; others had passed legislation forbidding it. The National Bank Act did nothing to alter this situation. It expressly stated that a bank formed under its provisions should not carry on business elsewhere than at the offices in places specified in its certificate of association. All that the law allowed was that State banks which had previously had branches should have the right to retain them if they came into the National Banking System.

The method of issuing notes against bond deposit instead of against commercial assets had shown weaknesses at a very early stage, as we have already intimated in a previous chapter. Its advantages became increasingly doubtful as time went on.

The obligation to tie up capital in a particular type of asset as a condition for the issue of notes made the volume of the note issue dependent in the long run on the profitability of these assets, and besides affecting the distribution of a bank's assets had reactions also on the form of its liabilities.

When note issue does not entail bond deposit, the bank has an unhindered choice in determining how much of the sight liabilities it can safely create against a given cash reserve shall be in the form of notes and how much in the form of deposit credits. Since both are payable on demand in legal tender, it would be a choice ruled by the public's preference for notes as against deposits which can be checked against, and it would be a matter of some indifference to the bank if it were suddenly called on by the public to vary the proportion between the two.

But if a bank is forced as a condition of note issue to invest in State bonds, it will, if these are unprofitable, be encouraged to get out its loans as far as possible by way of deposit credits rather than by the issue of notes.[1]

We must now examine the actual facts of the case as they presented themselves in America. State bonds, being as they

---

[1] It has sometimes been supposed, on an analogy with the English system, that by controlling the amount of note issue, control was at the same time established over the total amount of bank credit created. But the analogy was incomplete. In England, Bank of England notes formed the legal tender cash of the other banks. In the case of a National Bank the bank's own notes were not legal tender cash. It was liable to pay cash for notes equally with deposits, and it was against the two together that it had to provide adequate cash reserves and the numerical relation between them was flexible within wide limits. The danger was that the banks might overstep these limits and find themselves with a level of deposits involving a much higher demand for hand-to-hand currency than they had the means to supply.

were in great demand as a basis for the note issue and at the same time a decreasing rather than an increasing amount on the market, generally stood at a premium. This factor, together with the provision by which a bank could only issue notes to the extent of 90 percent of the face value of the bonds it purchased, greatly reduced the profitability of locking up funds in these bonds for the purpose of obtaining notes, and where a bank could get out its loans otherwise than by notes, it naturally preferred to do so. This caused variations from district to district as well as from year to year, and tended to increase deposit credits disproportionately to the increase in the note issue. In parts of the country where people insisted on having notes, banks charged a higher rate of interest than in those parts of the country where borrowers could be induced to take deposit credits and where check payments predominated over demands for currency withdrawals in the form of notes.

Looking at the long period movements in the circulation we find that between the inception of the National Banking System and 1900 they exhibit a trend which cannot but be considered as exceptional if compared with that of the note issues in other countries not working on a bond deposit basis. At the beginning of the 'eighties the Federal Government began to reduce its indebtedness by paying off its bonds; so that a scarcity of note-backing medium arose, and what there was stood at a high premium and gave a correspondingly small return. There consequently ensued a rapid reduction in the National Bank circulation outstanding, and between 1881 and 1890 there was a decrease of some 60 percent. During the whole of the period, when notes were diminishing or practically constant in volume, there was on the other hand a rapid increase of bank reserves of cash (chiefly of specie; legal tender notes remained a fairly constant element), and also a steady increase in deposits. This was quite contrary to what would be expected under an ordinary asset currency, where inflows of specie, whether from abroad or from internal hoards, are accompanied by increases in note issues.

A great deal of comment was also raised by the inelasticity exhibited by the note issue in the short run. The fluctuations shown under an ordinary system in the proportion between note and deposit liabilities, especially in response to seasonal changes in demand, found no parallel in America in spite of its large agricultural interest and heavy crop-moving demands for cash. The failure of the note circulation to respond to these demands intensified the autumnal strain on the money market and the banking system.

The explanation of the inflexibility of the note circulation lay as much in its lack of contractibility as in its lack of expansibility. It was expensive and slow to negotiate the purchase of new bonds in order to obtain additional notes from the Comptroller when the need arose, and the incentive to do so was further diminished by the fact that the notes could only be retired after the need had passed, by going through the same formalities and expense. Moreover, there was a legal limit on the number of notes that might be retired in any one month.[2] Notes once taken out by any bank were usually used by that bank to the full extent. It did not keep but a very small proportion on hand for periods of extra heavy demand for hand-to-hand currency, and so, in times when such demands arose, the banks could only meet them by drawing on their cash reserves and paying out legal tender, and they were pressed to a sharp restriction of credits all round in order to meet their obligations.

The lack of any reserve of notes led to frequent and violent fluctuations in interest rates. There was every year a steep rise in the autumn.

The popular illusion that the securing of notes by bond

---

[2] $3,000,000 up to 1908 and after that $9,000,000.

deposit would guarantee that they would always be paid in full had been dispelled. Later observers came, moreover, to realise that the system was responsible for suppressing some of the natural checks to over-expansions. It made the return of notes to the issuing bank for redemption in the ordinary course of business very infrequent. The uniformity of the form of the notes of different banks, as well as the semblance of indubitable security with which they were endowed by the law, caused the public to regard the notes of one bank as being as good as those of any other. More important still was the failure of the banks reciprocally to return each other's notes. Instead of sending in the notes of its rivals for clearance, a bank usually paid them out again over its own counter. This was due, in the first place, to the trouble and expense involved in sending notes back to the redeeming agencies which, in the absence of branch banking, were few and far between,[3] and in the second place, to the absence of any immediate incentive, in view of the costliness of the issue, for a bank to replace foreign notes by its own. These circumstances removed one of the tests which warns a bank when it is over-expanding by drawing on its reserves at an early stage.

A series of acute financial crises occurred in fairly quick succession—1873, 1884, 1890, 1893, 1907. Crises occurred on most of these occasions in London as well, but they were nothing like as stringent. Money rates in New York rose to fantastic heights as compared with London, and there was one other even more marked dissimilarity. In America there took place in three out of the five cases (1873, 1893 and 1907) widespread suspensions of cash payments, either partial or complete, with currency at a premium over claims on banking accounts. These tendencies culminated in the crisis of

[3] Up to 1874 notes were redeemable at the counter of the issuing bank and at some bank in one of the cities designated as redemption cities. After 1874 they were redeemable at the bank's own counter and at the Treasury.

1907, when suspensions lasted in some measure for a period of over two months.

There had been for some time a growing dissatisfaction with the fundamentals of the American system. The most obvious distinguishing feature, and the one to which attention was first directed, was of course the method of note issue, and some of the critics believed that the defect was connected solely with this system of issue against bond deposit, and that it would not be present under an ordinary asset currency. Its failings were summarised under the term "inelasticity." This is a term which has frequently had a dangerous connotation, being more often than not a cloak for the advocacy of inflation, but, as we have already explained in a previous section, there was some justification in the American case for the accusation that the note issue lacked necessary elasticity. It failed to provide for fluctuating demands for cash, firstly with seasonal, and secondly with crisis needs. It was the deficiency in supplying the latter that was given most prominence. The problem was how to provide an "emergency currency."

It was observed after 1879[4] that it was chiefly pressure exerted on the banks by depositors to withdraw hand-to-hand cash and not by note-holders to withdraw legal tender money that precipitated suspensions. It was contended, not unreasonably by the banks that their suspensions were the direct result of their being unable to issue extra notes. If they had been able to do this, they could have satisfied the demands of their depositors for cash by giving them notes, and in these circumstances the demand of customers for cash, both in the narrower sense *and* in the wider sense (that is, in the sense of paying out legal tender for either notes or deposits if and when demanded), could have been maintained. The demand of the public was only to change the form of

---

[4] The date when specie payments were resumed.

the medium—from deposits to notes: they wanted simply hand-to-hand currency and would have been as well satisfied with bank-notes as with legal tender. Reserves of legal tender could then have been kept practically intact—the additional note-holders would not have drawn on them; but as it was in the face of the inability to issue notes, the demand for cash by the depositors could only be satisfied if at all out of the reserves of legal tender, and these would soon have been exhausted. The suspension of cash payments was, according to this view, due to the lack of variability in the *form* of the currency (current accounts to notes).[5]

Some attempts were made to remedy the situation along the lines of this argument. It had been suggested by the promoters of what was known as the Baltimore Plan in 1894 that the bond deposit system should be abandoned altogether in favour of an ordinary asset currency accompanied by a safety fund guarantee. This proposal was, however, never taken up very enthusiastically. In 1900 measures were introduced to make the note issue more profitable. An Act was passed to allow banks to take out notes equal in value to the full face value of the bonds they deposited instead of only to 90 percent of that value, and the tax on the note issue was reduced from 1 percent to ½ percent. After 1900, too, the Secretary of the Treasury interpreted the

[5] The Comptroller of the Currency in his report for 1907 (pp. 73–4) remarks: "The only way in which bank credits can be properly protected from sudden and unexpected calls, when all may be involved at the same time, is by a system of note credits which can be at any time immediately exchanged for the deposit credits. They are essentially the same thing, and should be daily and hourly if necessary, convertible from one to the other at the option of the creditor who is the depositor or note-holder. The bank of issue should be required, and must in self-defence, keep the same reserves against notes as against deposits. If this is done, there is no expansion or inflation when a note is paid out to a depositor and no contraction when a note is returned to the bank for deposit. With a given amount of reserve money a given total of deposits and notes can be maintained, and it makes no difference to the bank or anyone else but the customer who uses either at his option, whether the deposit remains in the bank as a credit to be checked against or is taken away in the shape of a circulating note."

law in a very liberal way and accepted municipal and other stocks for note backing where previously only strictly Government securities had been eligible. The object of this step was to increase the circulation in the autumn to meet the demands of crop moving. It was intended to be purely a temporary seasonal increase, but failed to serve this purpose because the circulation did not contract again after the seasonal demand for cash had fallen off, and so there was in the next year just the same lack of provision for the autumnal cash drain as before. In general, these measures served only to make a permanent increase in the circulation without increasing its short period elasticity. It still left no slack ready to be taken up in an emergency. The result was merely a progressive increase in the circulation between 1900 and 1907 of over 90 percent, which provided currency for the inflationary boom of those years. As was evidenced by the events of 1907, the bond deposit system had proved incapable of modification in the direction of providing increased bank currency for emergencies.

Other attempts at interpreting the cause of the difficulties laid less stress on the question of note issues and sought the primary explanation more in other features of the American structure. One of these was the system of legal reserve ratios.[6] So far as the possibilities of credit expansion were concerned, the requirements of minimum reserve ratios probably did not cause the banks to expand less than they otherwise would; the legal minimum was a good deal below what the banks of their own accord thought fit to keep in

[6] Up to 1874 National Banks in New York had to hold in lawful money in their own vaults 25 percent of deposits plus circulation. Banks in other cities designated "redemption" cities or "reserve" cities as they were later called, must also hold 25 percent, but half of this might be held on deposit in New York. All other banks had to keep 15 percent, of which three-fifths might be on deposit with approved banks in any of the "reserve" cities. After 1874 this legal reserve requirement was revised to apply to deposits only and not to note circulation as well. After 1887 Chicago and St. Louis were given the position of "central reserve" cities, the same as New York.

normal times. But immediately the sort of event occurred for the very purpose of which such reserves should be kept, namely, an extra heavy demand for cash, the banks could only use their reserves to a very small extent before they approached the legal minimum. If they were not to be allowed to fall below the legal minimum, there was very little slack for taking up in times of pressure. So if deposits were being withdrawn rather more rapidly than usual, the situation could only be met by immediately calling in loans, thus cancelling some deposits and thereby diminishing the total amount of necessary reserve money. Such a procedure forces as much liquidation as if the banks were without cash reserves, and if the process is at all general, affecting a large number of banks, the liquidity of the individual bank is lost in the liquidity of the whole system.

The banks were faced with these alternatives: either they could suspend cash payments immediately, or they could use their cash reserves as far as possible to meet current demands in the hope of stemming the demand for cash and rendering such a suspension unnecessary. Under the American law a bank falling below its legal reserve requirements was obliged to discontinue lending operations until the deficit had been made good. This enforced on the banks endeavouring to maintain cash payments in the crisis a policy of immediate loan contraction. Given the choice, then, between falling below legal reserve requirements and suspending payments immediately, it was a much easier way out for the banks to choose the latter course. Such a procedure stopped the claims of depositors and made it possible for the banks to give their debtor customers time to repay their loans and even to give new loans so far as people were still willing to take payment in uncashable checks, or (in the case where payments were still made on a certain percentage of deposits) in partly cashable checks. The banks might find that this policy promised more likelihood of their customers being able to pay back their loans in the end than if they immediately caused them to go into liquidation.

At all events, the banks seemed to have suspended payments immediately as they approached the legal reserve limit, which means while they were still in a very strong reserve position. The figures of the reserve positions, given in the Annual Reports of the Comptroller of the Currency, are averages for all the banks in each State or Reserve City, and so cover up the individual movements, but it seems fairly certain that the banks did not in many cases allow their reserves ratios to go below the legal limit to any significant extent. The action of the banks in suspending payments was technically, of course, an act of insolvency, but this was given official sanction in a number of ways and a long tradition of wholesale suspensions both before and after the inception of the National Banking System had accustomed the public to their legality. The Comptroller allowed the banks to restrict payments for a period of several months on end and then permitted them to resume business as long as he considered their assets were "sound." This happened in some cases even after a bank had been put into the hands of a receiver in bankruptcy.[7] The circumstances in which the banks resorted to suspensions lent a good deal of support to the view that it was primarily an elastic reserve policy rather than an elastic currency that was in urgent need.[8]

A third line of argument laid emphasis on the necessity for some rearrangement in the existing system of holding and utilising reserve funds. At a very early stage the practice had developed among the country banks of depositing balances, which they counted as equivalent to cash, with banks in the large cities. They kept on an average about half of their total reserves on redeposit in this way and about half

[7] E.g., see "Report of the Comptroller of the Currency," 1891–2, p. 36.
[8] E.g., see Sprague, "Banking Reform," 1910, p. 68.

in their own vaults.[9] The banks in "redemption" cities or "reserve" and "central reserve" cities, as they were later designated, were officially recognised as being in a special category as bankers' banks by the National Banking Law. The conspicuous position held by the banks of New York city in this respect—in 1912 six or seven of them held between them about three-quarters of all the bankers' balances—seemed to point to the existence of spontaneous tendencies to the pyramiding and centralisation of reserves and the natural development of a quasi-central banking agency, even if one is not superimposed.

The position as it stood was regarded as exceedingly unsatisfactory. It had been a frequent complaint in financial circles ever since 1857 that the practice of re-deposit by the country banks with the city banks, and more particularly with the banks in New York City, encouraged by a number of these banks who paid interest on demand deposits, gave an unhealthy stimulus to speculation on the Stock Exchange by flooding the call loan market with cheap accommodation. It was, what is more important, nearly always the demands for withdrawals of these bankers' balances by their country owners which precipitated crises in the financial system of the country.

The development of the debtor position of one group of banks, the town banks, to the other group, the country banks, and the extreme instability of this element in the financial structure, is one which would probably have been unimportant if there had been branch banking. The absence of branch organisation may have tended somewhat to raise the level of the amount of call loan money, and it most certainly made it more unstable than it would have been with branch organisation.

The difficulties of a unit bank as compared with a branch

---

[9] See Laughlin, "Banking Reform," pp. 199 ff.

system in diversifying risks both in its assets as well as in its deposit liabilities was partly compensatable by the possibility open to the country banks of putting funds on deposit with a town bank and so indirectly taking advantage of the opportunities for investment offered by the money market. The country banks regarded these deposits as their second line of defence—as part of their liquid funds which they would be able to withdraw immediately the demands for cash from their customers increased, as happened regularly in the crop-moving season, and they were given official recognition as such by the provision of the National Bank Act, which allowed such deposits to be counted by the country banks as a certain portion of their legal reserves. It is not denied that under a branch system funds from the country would still find their way to the call loan market via the head office or town branches of the parent bank, but the much more restricted range of alternative investments available to one bank in a unit system probably caused rather more to seek this particular outlet.

The unit system with the practice of re-deposit showed great susceptibility to the spread of panic both in the case where the originating disturbance started in the affairs of a country bank, and in the case where it arose at the city bank end. Firstly, a country bank in a unit system is less able to obtain funds from outside when it is under pressure. It may, it is true, be able to borrow from another bank, but this is more difficult and takes longer to negotiate than a transfer of funds from the cash reserves of other branches of the same bank, and it is the ability to obtain funds *in time* that is important in order to stop the loss of confidence among the public which leads to a panic run liable to spread to other banks as well. A single weak spot in the system is less likely to affect the whole system under branch organisation than under unit organisation.

Secondly, the call loan position in New York was rendered

exceedingly vulnerable in the event of extra heavy demands for withdrawals, and especially in the circumstances associated with the break of a boom when call loans proved to be among the most illiquid of assets. Experience taught the country banks that their correspondents in New York found it difficult to cash their deposits in such a situation. Consequently, immediately the slightest indication of defect occurred, there was a scramble by the country banks to withdraw their balances *en bloc* from New York. The fear that they would in a few days' time find their balances frozen led them to withdraw them immediately, whether they were actually in need of cash themselves or not. Those banks who got their balances out in time were often found on such occasions to have far larger reserves of cash in vaults than at periods of less acute demand from the public. The New York banks were driven to suspend payment, and those country banks who had not withdrawn their funds in time had to suspend also.

The difference in a branch system would be, not that there would not still occur a flow of funds from the interior of New York, but that the greater part of these funds would be disposed of by the town branches or head offices of the banks remitting them, and each bank would retain direct control over its own reserves.[10] And in a period of pressure, branches would not attempt to withdraw all the spare funds from their head office, regardless of whether they needed them or not. There would be a concentration of funds on points where they were needed most to satisfy the demands of customers and stop a run.

It was realised in some quarters that many of the difficulties could have been remedied by the institution of branch

---

[10] It is not likely that banks would deposit with each other except in so far as it might be necessary for one bank to keep balances in a place where it had no branch for making payments in that place. The amount of such balances would normally be small.

banking along Canadian lines, but this was regarded as a political impossibility, and so attention was turned to the more practical expedient of finding some systematic means of the more economical utilisation of reserves in a crisis within the general framework of the existing system.

It seemed increasingly apparent that it was impossible to rely on the independent and unaided efforts of the banks to secure this end. Some attempts of a somewhat unsystematic nature had already been made by them. One of these was the use of the clearing-house loan certificate.[11] This was a practice which had been started by the banks of New York and the banks of Boston in 1860. A majority of the banks belonging to the Clearing House Association entered into an agreement under which, when a bank had an adverse clearing balance, it should, instead of paying cash to the creditor bank, deposit collateral with the Clearing House Association, against which the latter should issue clearing-house loan certificates to be received in payment by the creditor bank. The certificates bore interest at a fairly high rate, varying from 5 to 10 percent, which went to the creditor bank holding them in lieu of balances owed. The essence of the scheme was that the banks in a strong position (with favourable clearing balances) should make loans to those in a weaker position (with unfavourable clearing-house balances). It was intended to prevent each bank trying to strengthen its position at the expense of the others, because without such an arrangement, no bank could extend its lending operations and all were induced to contract because of the fear of losing reserves to other banks at a time when the demand of the public for cash was increasing. On the first occasion that the clearing-house loan certificate device was used by the New York banks it was accompanied by an agreement for treating the specie reserves of all banks as a

[11] Cf. Sprague, "Crises under the National Banking System" (U.S.A. National Monetary Commission).

common fund so that the banks having to bear the greatest strain not from other banks, but from the claims of the public, should be able to draw on the reserves of banks less subject to such strain. This pooling of reserves, or "reserve equalisation" as it was called, meant that it was quite impossible for a bank to affect its individual reserve position by contracting its loans.

In the 1860 crisis the banks in both Boston and New York succeeded in maintaining cash payments with the aid of the loan certificate. In the 1873 crisis the device was used again, this time by the clearing-house associations in no less than seven of the principal cities. It did not succeed in averting entirely a suspension of cash payments, but the suspension lasted the comparatively short period of less than three weeks.

In subsequent crises the clearing-house loan certificates were used by the associations in nearly all the leading cities, but without the equalisation of reserves. The banks could not reach agreement to pool their reserves in these later crises. Those of 1884 and 1890 were, however, slight, and the banks did not suspend, but in 1893 and 1907 the use of clearing-house loan certificates, without the equalisation of reserves, itself led almost immediately to suspension.

The issue of certificates without the equalisation of reserves proved fatal to individual banks. A bank which received a large number of checks drawn on other banks from customers who wanted to withdraw cash, experienced heavy drains on their reserves. At the same time they might have favourable clearing-house balances with other banks (those on which the checks were drawn) but be unable to obtain any cash from these banks on account of the clearing-house arrangement, while these other banks might be exceptionally strong in cash reserves because customers did not happen to be drawing directly on them for cash. The banks which were subjected to the heavy demand for cash by the public, or the country banks, as the case might be, tried to sidetrack this effect of the clearing-house agreement by encouraging their customers to take checks for cash direct to the banks on which they were drawn instead of handing them into their own banks for settlement in the clearings. This was, however, impossible to do beyond a certain measure; the banks adversely affected by the issue of the loan certificates had to suspend payment; this started a run on the others and they suspended also.

Both the successes and the failures of the clearing-house loan certificate device gave force to the conclusion, firstly, that there should be somewhere an adequate reserve of lending power for use in the crisis, and, secondly, that this should be available for the collective benefit of all banks. Further, the idea was gaining ground that it could only be provided by an organisation in some manner aloof from the operations of ordinary commercial banks. It must be a bank that was in normal times not fully "lent up."

Some such sort of relief during a crisis had been provided by the Treasury. The principle had been established in 1846 that the Treasury should be independent of the banks, that is, that it should keep its own surplus funds instead of depositing them with the banks. It was objected that this had an inconvenient effect on the money market if collections exceeded disbursements for any length of time, because in that case it caused sudden withdrawals and returns of funds from and to the market; and from the time of the Civil War onwards the Independent Treasury System was not strictly preserved. The Treasury began depositing funds in selected National Banks and adopted the practice of giving relief in times of crisis. The methods of using its funds in a way to make the money market more liquid were various.[12] As early as 1857, even before the National Banking System had

---

[12] See U.S. National Monetary Commission—"The Independent Treasury."

come into being, it had helped the market by purchasing bonds. In 1873 it again bought bonds and also sold $5,000,000 of gold, the proceeds of which it put on deposit in certain banks. In 1884 it prepaid some of the interest on the public debt. In 1890 it again prepaid interest and bought bonds. In 1893 the Treasury was unable to give any aid at all; it actually had a deficit and needed to borrow itself from the banks. In 1907 it transferred some funds to the banks, but the amount it had on hand was small, since it had already deposited most of its surplus with them before the crisis.

The Treasury had thus been undertaking some of the functions of a central bank by carrying out what was equivalent to open market operations (purchases of securities) and by lending directly to the banks. The rather fortuitous nature of this kind of relief led bank reformers to demand a more "scientific" mode of relief in crises. It was only a lucky chance if the Treasury happened to have surpluses at the time when the crisis came. There was, on the other hand, a considerable body of opinion which denounced the Treasury relief on the grounds that it gave an impetus to expansion. Banks expected to receive assistance if they got into difficulties, and therefore expanded on the basis of these anticipations.

It became also part of the positive programme for banking reform that it should provide for an institution which could act as the Government's fiscal agent.[13] The Treasury experiences during the course of the previous century, both of the system of keeping its own funds and of the system of depositing them with various State or National Banks at the risk of not being able to obtain them in the event of the failure of these banks, had directed attention towards the possibility of finding some depositary which was free from the objections of both these systems. In other countries the necessary services were performed by the Central Bank.

---

[13] Cf. Parker Willis, "The Federal Reserve System," Book I., Chapter 2.

One other feature of the American system which the reformers hoped to remedy was the high cost of check collection. The majority of the banks in America were in the habit of making a charge known as the "exchange" charge for paying their own checks. This charge purported to cover the cost of providing funds to pay the check in a distant place because the bank had either to shift currency or to maintain a balance in a distant centre. What the banks were actually able to charge was probably much above the real expense involved, but there is little doubt that there was room in the old system for a considerable reduction in the real cost of check collection by reducing the necessary amount of transmission of funds.[14]

It was the crisis of 1907 which gave the final impetus to the growing agitation for banking reform, but there was still a difference of opinion as to whether the chief fault lay with the system of note issue or with the lack of branch organisation or with the legal reserve regulations. On the whole, there was a strong majority in favour of the introduction of some kind of co-operative organisation of existing banks for the purpose of providing reserve funds for panic financiering. Authoritative support was given to the suggestion that the necessary changes could best be made through the establishment of a central bank of issue and reserve.[15] But even after the 1907 crisis there was still a good deal of opposition to the introduction of real central banking, and the idea persisted that a purely emergency organisation for "relief"

[14] It was part of the services of the Federal Reserve System to secure the payment of checks at par. The twelve Federal Reserve Banks and their branches hold the reserves of the member banks, and these act as clearing balances. Checks can be presented at the nearest Federal Reserve Bank, and if the check is drawn on a bank which is a member of the same Federal Reserve district, funds are already available. Where checks move out of the district, the Federal Reserve Bank pays the cost of any necessary currency shipments. The system also exerts pressure on non-member banks because Federal Reserve Banks will not collect checks on banks which refuse to clear at par.

[15] See "Report of the Comptroller of the Currency," 1907, pp. 71–79.

would meet the case. This was the attitude behind the Aldrich-Vreeland Act of 1908, which provided for the issue of emergency currency against securities other than United States Bonds and adopted commercial bills as a basis for note issue for the first time. The Act authorised banks to form voluntary associations under the arrangement that a bank belonging to such an association could deposit with it any securities (including commercial bills) against which it might receive additional notes. All the banks belonging to the association were then jointly and severally liable for the redemption of the additional circulation. National Banks were also given the option of applying to the Comptroller of the Currency for additional notes secured by assets other than United States Bonds.

The same Act set up the National Monetary Commission to report on banking reform. The Commission sat four years and carried out investigations, not only into the details of the American system, but also into the experiences and practices of European countries with central banks. The fact that these countries had escaped general suspensions of cash payments was attributed to the strength of the central institutions, the concentration and mobilisation of reserves and the prompt use of these reserves in a crisis. Stress was, moreover, placed on the part played by these central banks of issue in regulating the money market via the discount system.[16] The influence of the publications of the Commission was to turn the favour of the reformers towards a permanent central organisation which should issue a currency based on gold and commercial paper, act as a lender of last resort and control the credit situation through the bank rate and open market dealings.

[16] See, for example, "The Discount System in Europe," by Paul M. Warburg (U.S. Monetary Commission). See also "Interviews on the Banking and Currency Systems of England, Scotland, France, Germany, Switzerland and Italy" (U.S. Monetary Commission).

The final outcome of the recommendations was the creation of the Federal Reserve System. Its organisation differed considerably from the European central bank: it consisted of twelve regional Federal Reserve Banks in the ownership of which those banks who became members of the system— and membership was compulsory on all National Banks— took a share by contributing to their capital. On these, under the guidance of the Federal Reserve Board, there devolved the tasks of issuing notes, keeping the reserves of the member banks and acting as lending agency to them by rediscounting.

A retrospective consideration of the background and circumstances of the foundation of the Federal Reserve System would seem to suggest that many, perhaps most, of the defects of American banking could, in principle, have been more naturally remedied otherwise than by the establishment of a central bank; that it was not the absence of a central bank *per se* that was at the root of the evil, and that, although this was admittedly a partial remedy for things for which other remedies were politically or technically impossible of realisation, there remained certain fundamental defects which could not be entirely, or in any great measure, overcome by the Federal Reserve System.

CHAPTER XII

The Arguments in Favour of Central Banking Reconsidered

It has been the purpose of the preceding chapters to elucidate the reasons, historical as well as logical, for the growth
of the form of bank organisation which we now call central
banking. Its origin is to be found in the establishment of
monopolies, either partial or complete, in the note issue.
Monopolies in this sphere outlasted the abolition of protectionism in other branches of economic activity. Those which
had been in existence prior to the growth of free trade doctrine were retained and reinforced: new creations occurred
where they had not previously existed.

Looking at the circumstances in which most of them were
established, we find that the early ones were founded for
political reasons connected with the exigencies of State finance, and no economic reason for allowing or disallowing
free entry into the note-issuing trade was, or could have
been given at that time, but once established, the monopolies persisted right up to and beyond the time when their
economic justification did at last come to be questioned. The
verdict of the discussions round this problem vindicated the
choice in favour of unity or monopoly in the note issue as
opposed to competition, and thereafter the superiority of

central banking over the alternative system became a dogma which never again came up for discussion and was accepted without question or comment in all the later foundations of central banks. In this chapter we shall recall and examine the main points in the defence of central banking against its logical alternative in an attempt to weigh up the evidence and to judge whether or not it is conclusive.

It may be useful first to recapitulate the broad differences in the characteristics of the two alternative systems. The primary definition of central banking is a banking system in which a single bank has either a complete or a residuary monopoly in the note issue. A residuary monopoly denotes a case where there are a number of note issuers, but all of these except one are working under narrow limitations, and this one authority is responsible for the bulk of the circulation, and is the sole bank possessing that measure of elasticity in its note issue which gives it the power to exercise control over the total amount of currency and credit available.

It was out of monopolies in the note issue that were derived the secondary functions and characteristics of our modern central banks. The guardianship of the bulk of the gold reserves of the banking system is obviously an accompaniment of the monopoly in the note issue: the holding of a large proportion of the bankers' cash reserves is also bound up with the same factor—it is a matter of convenience for the banks to keep their surplus balances at the central bank but it is safe for them to entrust a major part of their cash reserves to a single outside establishment only if they can be absolutely certain that this authority will be able in all circumstances to pay out such reserves in a medium which will be always acceptable to the public. This can only be guaranteed if the notes of this authority can be given forced currency in time of need. Last, but not least, control over the note issue gives the central bank power to exercise control over the general credit situation. These considerations justify us in using the term "central banking" to cover the narrower as well as the wider concept.

A central bank is not a natural product of banking development. It is imposed from outside or comes into being as the result of Government favours. This factor is responsible for marked effects on the whole currency and credit structure which brings it into sharp contrast with what would happen under a system of free banking from which Government protection was absent.

"Free banking"[1] denotes a *régime* where note-issuing banks are allowed to set up in the same way as any other type of business enterprise, so long as they comply with the general company law. The requirement for their establishment is not special conditional authorisation from a Government authority, but the ability to raise sufficient capital, and public confidence, to gain acceptance for their notes and ensure the profitability of the undertaking. Under such a system all banks would not only be allowed the same rights, but would also be subjected to the same responsibilities as other business enterprises. If they failed to meet their obligations they would be declared bankrupt and put into liquidation, and their assets used to meet the claims of their creditors, in which case the shareholders would lose the whole or part of their capital, and the penalty for failure would be paid, at least for the most part, by those responsible for the policy of the bank. Notes issued under this system would be "promises to pay," and such obligations must be met on demand in the generally accepted medium which

[1] It must be understood that the use of the term "free banking" in the subsequent analysis is not synonymous with that particular system of so-called free banking which was put into practice in the United States of America in the middle of last century. As was pointed out in the previous chapter, the American system was characterised by certain features which render it quite inappropriate as an example of the working of free banking in the more general sense.

we will assume to be gold. No bank would have the right to call on the Government or on any other institution for special help in time of need. No bank would be able to give its notes forced currency by declaring them to be legal tender for all payments, and it is unlikely that the public would accept inconvertible notes of any such bank except at a discount varying with the prospect of their again becoming convertible. A general abandonment of the gold standard is inconceivable under these conditions, and with a strict interpretation of the bankruptcy laws any bank suspending payments would at once be put into the hands of a receiver.

A central bank, on the other hand, being founded with the aid either direct or indirect of the Government, is able to fall back on the Government for protection from the disagreeable consequences of its acts. The central bank, which cannot meet its obligations, is allowed to suspend payment and to go off the gold standard, while its notes are given forced currency. The history of central banks is full of such legalised bankruptcies.[2]

In the natural development of a free-banking system there is no apparent reason why a single bank should acquire a position of hegemony in which the bulk of the gold and cash reserves of the banking community were concentrated in its hands. The dictum of Bagehot, that a centralised reserve system is entirely unnatural and that the natural system would be one where each bank kept its own reserves in its own vaults, has been challenged by reference to the position of New York as a reserve centre prior to 1913. We cannot doubt the tendencies to a concentration of balances on a considerable scale in financial centres, and under a unit banking system the out-of-town banks will carry deposits with the banks in such a centre. The extent of this holding of balances by some banks for the account of others would be

---

[2] Cf. W. Scharling, "Bankpolitik," pp. 337–8.

much smaller, however, were banks allowed to have their own branches where they chose. The balances that a bank finds it convenient to keep in the financial centre, would then generally be held by the bank's own branch in that city, where they would remain under its own control and management.

In a multiple system each bank must determine the volume of its note issue, or of its total demand liabilities, with a close watch on its reserve position, and it is to be expected that the total volume of credit a bank could safely leave outstanding would be very sensitive to changes in its reserve position. The central bank can, on the other hand, allow its reserve proportion to undergo large changes partly on account of the concentration of reserves and partly on the expectation that it will be released from its obligations, if it finds itself in difficulties.[3]

We can now turn to the analysis of the major points at issue between those who attacked free banking and those who defended it. Historically the free-banking case was connected predominantly with those theories of currency and credit which were sponsored by the banking school, and the central banking case was likewise, but perhaps a little less closely, linked up with the theories of the currency school. It was not true in all instances that a member of the free-banking school supported the one and a member of the central banking school the other, but because this was true in the majority of cases, the success of the currency school was claimed as a victory for the central banking school as well. Actually the second controversy could be judged independently of the first and should be regarded as distinct. We shall not deal here in detail with the contents of the rival theses in the banking *versus* currency controversy, which are fairly familiar ground. It will suffice to remark how far

[3] Cf. footnote 32 on p. 194 of this chapter.

the link with the banking *versus* currency controversy weighted the evidence in the free banking *versus* central banking controversy.

The circumstance that the free-banking school, especially in France, placed so much emphasis on that part of their argument which sprang from the theories of the banking school, tended, it is true, to cast suspicion on the free-banking case. A not inconsiderable number of the free bankers denied the quantity theory of money, and promoted ideas that were of an obtrusively inflationary character. It may be recalled that according to this school no such thing as an over-issue of bank-notes can take place so long as they are only issued in response to the "needs of trade" and continuous convertibility is maintained. It was their contention that so long as notes are issued on short-term loan (or so long as the assets of note-issuing banks are *"bankmässige"*) they cannot be issued in excess. The demand for loans, and therefore for notes, will be confined to limits imposed by the profitability of borrowing. Should the issue be found to be in excess of the needs of trade, notes will come back to the bank in repayment of loans falling due and for which there will be no demand for renewal; they will consequently be automatically withdrawn from the circulation. It was also a prevalent idea that since there is no restriction on the creation of credit by way of bills of exchange in ordinary commercial dealings, it is inconsistent to place a limit on that particular mode of lending which takes place via the note issue. If the banks issue notes with which they discount bills of exchange, they are merely changing the form of the lending. Since the bills would have existed in any case, the banks made no net addition to the total volume of credit.

Notes issued on short-term loan, the argument continues, become only temporarily part of the circulation, and this was held to constitute a vital distinction between bank-notes which had an automatic reflux and "pure paper money" which, instead of being paid out by way of short-term loan, was permanently released in payment for goods and services. Real paper money made a permanent addition to the amount of the circulation, and neither was its quantity controlled by the needs of trade. It therefore exerted a marked and lasting influence on prices. In the case of bank-notes, the flowback after the expiry of the term of the loan served also a second purpose by providing safeguards for the maintenance of continuous convertibility, since at the time of such repayments either the note issue was decreased or the gold reserves were increased.

It has been pointed out, in criticism of this doctrine, that it failed to perceive that borrowing on bills of exchange or on any other security will not be a given quantity fixed independently of bank policy, but will be a function of the rate of interest charged, and can be expanded indefinitely, provided the banks offer a low enough rate. Secondly, if the banking school argued that the principle of "*bankmässige Deckung*" provided against all dangerous contingencies, such as a threat to reserves and therefore to convertibility, simply because notes were always only temporarily issued and could be withdrawn at short notice, they ignored the truth that an over-issue even for so short a period as the normal *échéance* of bills of exchange cannot (if it is general to a majority of banks in the case of a free-banking system, and without qualification in a unitary banking system) be suddenly rectified without causing all those effects characteristic of a credit contraction which are to be regarded as the evil aftermath of any over-issue. A net reduction of loans cannot take place without causing disturbances both in the financial and in the industrial structure. One bank can only make heavy reductions without causing widespread liquidations and losses in the system if another bank will lend to fill the gap. It is a matter of shifting, and the whole system cannot shift at the same time. The mere fact that the banks' loans are on short term does not mean that a credit contraction can take place in the nick of time without causing just those disturbances which the currency school aimed at preventing.

There remains, however, one point connected with the principle of *"bankmässige Deckung"* and the automatic reflux of notes which might have a certain validity in a free-banking system which it could not have in a centralised system of note issue. This point relates to the possibility of the mutual control between banks operating as a check on over-issue. In a multiple system of issue the notes of any individual bank will be continually flowing into other banks and cleared. Now the shorter the period for which loans are made, the more frequent will be the repayment of outstanding loans; and the larger the proportion of total loans outstanding that are coming forward for repayment each day, the larger will be the proportion of the outstanding note issue coming into the banks on any day. If we suppose that one bank starts to expand while other banks maintain only the same issues as before, the flow of adverse claims required to be met in gold by the former through the clearings will be affected by the shorter or longer length of the term for which loans are made. How far this mechanism can be effective as a break on over-issues we shall discuss in a later section of this chapter.[4]

The currency school intended to make the total circulation vary with outflows and inflows of gold in the supposed manner of purely metallic currency. They thought that this end could be accomplished by fixing the fiduciary note issue. Their error was to have ignored the fundamental similarity of deposit credits to the issue of notes. This error would not have been crucial in so far as it concerned only the deposit credit creating facilities of the commercial

[4] See p. 179 ff.

banks.[5] In so far as these banks keep fairly constant ratios between their cash reserves and their deposit liabilities, the total volume of credit can be made to move in response to gold movements (its changes will be a fairly constant multiple of such movements), *provided the reserves of these banks are made to move in the same way as gold.* But this would require the fixing, not of the fiduciary note issue of the Bank of England but of the quantity not covered by gold, of its notes in circulation plus its deposit liabilities. As it is, the Bank of England can vary its lending and so alter the volume of deposits on its books to the credit of the commercial banks, and therefore the cash reserves of those banks, independently of gold movements, merely allowing the operation to affect its own reserve "proportion." It can do this within limits that are of course widened by the willingness of the Government to abrogate the Bank Act in case of emergency.

There were mistakes and omissions in the doctrines of both schools, and as they worked out in practice there seems not to be such a great deal of difference between the actual results secured by those who insisted that it was essential to impose some such rule as a fixed limitation on the amount of the fiduciary note issue, and those who believed that the only necessary regulation was that notes should be convertible into specie.

We may conclude that logically, in so far as the disagreement between the two parties free banking and central banking was based solely on the positions they took up with regard to the banking *versus* currency controversy, there is no definite ground for presumption in favour of either one or the other. It is, furthermore, true that, given the independent arguments in the free-banking case which we are

---

[5] There seems to be no generally recognised term to distinguish other banks from the central bank. We shall here use the term "commercial" to describe all banks other than the central bank.

about to examine, it was perfectly consistent for the currency school, in so far as their aim was to find a system in which there were checks on fluctuations in the volume of credit, to sponsor the free-banking case. Both Michaelis and Mises are in this position.

The decisive arguments, and those, therefore, on which the case can be exclusively discussed, are the arguments introduced by either side additional to, and independent of, the points at issue between the banking and currency schools. We shall, therefore, turn our attention to the major arguments of the free banking *versus* central banking controversy proper. The points that have been raised in defence of the one system or in condemnation of the other can be dealt with under five heads.

The first of these is an argument against free banking, which runs in the following terms. It is always to be expected under a multiple banking system that even if the general stability of the whole system is assured, there will be failures of individual banks from time to time, just as there occur bankruptcies among the firms in other industries. The notes of any bank do not stay in the hands of those people who are enabled to borrow from that bank and therefore directly benefit from its note issue. They are paid away into the hands of third parties who have no immediate connection with the bank concerned. Those people who happen to be in possession of the notes of the failed bank at the time of its failure will suffer loss. A large proportion of such notes is likely to be in the hands of those who are either too ignorant, or by reason of their subordinate position, unable, to refuse to accept the notes of a bank which a more informed or better-placed person would reject because of suspicion attaching to the affairs of that bank. In other words, there is placed on the community the burden of discriminating between good and bad notes, and it falls especially hard on those sections of the community who are least able to bear it. It is, therefore, concluded that the Government should intervene and protect the note-holder by introducing some uniformity into the note issue. In the last analysis this is an argument for spreading the risk evenly among all note-holders. Whether or not we accept it is not dependent on economic analysis, and it is a question which we cannot decide on scientific grounds. We can but call attention to the suggestion of the free bankers that the spreading of the risk could only be done at the expense of increasing the losses all round.

The second point and the one to which most attention has usually been devoted is the question of the relative probability of inflations of the currency leading up to the phenomena of crises and depressions. The central banking school supposed that under a free-banking system fluctuations in the volume of money and therefore in economic activity in general would be much more violent than in a system where there was a single note issuer. In a free-banking system competition among the banks would provoke a constant tendency to the lowering of discount rates and increases in the volume of credit It would be followed eventually by an external drain of gold, but this was a check which operated too late, because by the time the drain began to affect the banks' reserves the seeds of the depression had already been sown, and the crisis would only be made more intense by the sudden contraction of lending forced on the banks by the urge to protect their reserves.

It was further argued that any tendency to expansion would become cumulative, because it was useless for some banks, who might be more acutely conscious of the difficulties that would arise in the event of an expansion and the resulting pressure on reserves, to hold off from expanding. They could not hope for escape from the strain by pursuing a conservative policy while others were inflating. The reasoning on which this conclusion was based is the following. When the public starts to demand gold for export, they will not select the notes of the guilty banks and present these for payment. They will send in any notes that come into their hands, and the proportions in which the notes of the different banks will be returned will roughly correspond to the proportions the note issues of the individual banks bear to the total circulation. Hence the non-expanding banks have to bear part of the pressure resulting from the expansion of a rival bank. Should a non-expanding bank insist on retaining its former reserve ratio, it will be compelled as a result of the encroachment on its reserves to decrease its lending. If this happens, the expanding bank (or group of banks) can go on expanding and taking business away from its rivals until the latter are finally driven out of business and the former obtains a *de facto* monopoly. So whether the banks with the more conservative tendencies expanded or not, they could not help losing reserves, and if they did not expand, they would lose business. Consequently, the argument runs, they will, in the interests of self-preservation, be induced to join in the inflation.

The flaw in this argument is its failure to observe that as a result of continuous expansion by one group and continuous contraction by the other the proportion of the gold outflow falling on the expanding group must increase *pari passu*, and that the reserves of this group will be exhausted entirely before the conservative group has been driven out of business.

The argument so far considered refers only to the unreliability of a check on inflation by way of the presentation of notes to the banks for redemption by the public. The free-banking party laid particular stress on another check which they contended worked automatically through the reciprocal claims of the banks upon each other's reserves.[6] Any

---

[6] Professor Mises has recently defended free banking along these lines in his "Geldwertstabilisierung und Konjunkturpolitik," 1928. Professor Neisser has, in reply to Mises, taken up the counter argument that the "automatic mechanism"

bank will continually be receiving payments from customers either in payment of loans or in the form of cash being paid in on deposit. In a system where all banks are competitors for business, one bank will not be prepared to pay out over its own counter the notes of rival banks, but will return them to their issuers through the clearing process. It is therefore to be supposed that if one bank expands out of step with the rest, the clearing balances will go against it and its rivals will draw on its gold reserves to the extent of its adverse balance. This mechanism would work at a much earlier stage than the external drain of gold and would cause the reserves to feel the effects of expansion almost immediately. It is unlikely that all banks will decide in concert to decrease their reserve ratios, and the bigger the conservative group which is not desirous of so doing, the stronger will be the check of these on the expansion of the other group. A bank which contemplates an expansion has got to take into account not only the direct effect on its reserve ratio, which comes about in the first instance when it increases its issue against the same absolute total reserve as before, but also the indirect effect occasioned by the withdrawal of cash to other banks. The size of the addition it can afford to make to its loans on the basis of a given drop in its reserve ratio will be correspondingly reduced, and its action will react partly to the benefit of the other banks who secure an accretion to their reserves. While admitting that circumstances may occur in which the majority of the banks are willing to allow some reduction in their reserve ratios, it is unlikely that they will ever risk fluctuations of dimensions anything like as great as those which are viewed with comparative equanimity by the central bank.

The free bankers therefore submitted that under their system an over-expansion was not only not any more likely, but

of credit control does not, in most circumstances, work. See his article "Notenbankfreiheit?" in the *Weltwirtschaftliches Archiv.*, October, 1930.

even much less likely than under a central banking system. In the latter system all notes are issued by a single bank: this bank receives all payments in, in its own notes, and can always pay its own notes out again; it therefore neither gives nor receives claims on specie reserves so far as inter-bank claims are concerned. The only source of claims is the demand for gold by the public. The effect could be seen in the very much longer average period of circulation (less frequent redemption) of notes under a unit system as compared with a multiple system of note issues.

The central banking school alleges that inter-bank control via the clearing mechanism is largely an illusion, and only functions under very special circumstances. If one bank increases its issues by a given proportion, its business will increase in the same proportion, and therefore the larger amount of loan repayments it will have falling due in any week will give it the same number of claims on rival banks as they have on it, so that no differences arise in the clearings and no claims on reserves.

It was consequently denied that, failing recourse to the situation where the notes of any one bank circulate, not over the whole area, but only over a narrowly circumscribed area, in which case notes passing out of their area of issue would be sent in by the *public* for collection[7]—a case which is analogous to that of international exchanges and which raises objections of its own—there is any automatic check on the expansion of note issues in a multiple banking system.

The argument as stated and the illustrations[8] given in support of it take no account of a lag occurring between the increase in the circulation of the expanding bank (which we will call A) and the increase in its loan repayments. If we

[7] A case considered by Michaelis. See his article, "Noten und Depositen" in Faucher's "Vierteljahrschrift," 1865, p. 132.

[8] See Chapter VII., p. 85 ff.

assume such a lag which in practice must occur, there will be a drain in the first instance on A's reserves, though this will only be a temporary efflux, and at a later period, when A's loan repayments increase, there will be a return of these reserves to A.[9] It seems, therefore, that whether or not the clearing mechanism will act as a factor tending to check A's expansion will depend on whether or not A can stand the reduction in its reserves during this interim period.

It is always assumed that in the case of a deposit credit system, the clearing mechanism will function against a bank which expands out of step with others.[10] The only differences between the two cases would seem to be that the temporary withdrawals in the lag period will be more rapid in the check case than in the note case. All checks which are drawn on the additional deposit credit, as the borrower spends it, will be paid into the banks for clearance immediately, and those drawn in favour of people banking with other banks will give rise to cash claims on the expanding bank. *None* of the checks will remain out in circulation; *all* will pass through the clearings. In the case of the note issue, on the other hand, only a small part of the issue will come back from circulation to the banks—viz., those notes that come in via loan repayments or in the form of new deposits. Eventually the expanding bank would get back the reserves it previously lost in the deposit case no less than in the note

---

[9] It is immaterial to the general conclusion what assumption we make regarding the way in which the increased lending takes place. We may assume (a) that A gives out all the additional loans at the same date, and that they are all of the same *échéance*; (b) that it gives them all out at the same date, but that they are distributed over different periods of *échéance*; or (c) that it increases its loans gradually over a period of time. In all cases A receives back sooner or later the reserves it previously lost. See the illustration in an appendix to this chapter [pp. 197–200].

[10] The same principles apply in the case of an accretion of cash to one bank and the demonstration (cf. Phillips, "Bank Credit") that the bank in question cannot expand its loans to anything approaching the extent represented by the amount of liabilities the additional reserves would support on the basis of the old reserve ratio, because withdrawals of cash will take place to other banks.

case, but the clearing mechanism exerts a controlling effect because the bank cannot stand a heavy reduction of reserves in the interim period; it cannot wait until their return at a later date.

The difference is a matter of degree rather than of kind. Whether or not the check will operate in the note case will be dependent on the importance of the drain of cash during the lag period. That there must be some lag, whether we take the note case or the deposit case, is indisputable[11] unless we adopt the unreal assumption that all the additional loans are lent out only "over night." The existence of the lag presupposes merely that the additional loans do not mature at the next settlement day but only one or more settlements later, or that the shortest period for which the loans may be made cannot make their repayment coincide with the repayment of those old loans which are the next in time to be repaid. It must be supposed that the borrower makes use of the loan proceeds and therefore transfers of funds must have taken place between the time of borrowing and the time of repayment. The borrower must first use the funds to make a purchase and later realise them again by making a sale. The purchases which the new borrowers make will partly provide the funds out of which previous borrowers, whose loans are falling due, make their repayments to the banks. At a later date other borrowers will provide the funds out of which our so-called new borrowers again become liquid and can pay back their loans. The most rapid rate at which such transactions can proceed must allow at least one settlement to take place in which the effect of the increased circulation of the expanding bank becomes apparent in the clearing balances, but has as yet no effect on the volume of loans falling due for repayment.

---

[11] Neisser seems to have neglected this factor, although he would need to assume it in order to prove that there is a basis for distinction between the check case and the note case; cf. his article, pp. 454–5.

We can make various assumptions about the term of the old and the new loans. If the term of loans is on the average increased with an increase in their volume, the lag period will be longer than if this is not the case. There seems no reason for assuming that the length of the lag will be any greater under the system of loan by deposit credit than under the system of lending in the form of notes. The only difference is that the size of the temporary drain will be larger in the deposit case than in the note case. Even allowing for the fact that some additional notes will find their way into the banks at an early stage in the form of new deposits by customers as well as by way of current loan repayments, it remains true that this is extremely unlikely to approach anywhere near the extent of the return of checks. It is possible, however, that the drain of cash caused by the reflux of notes to other banks during the lag period may still be sufficient to act as a deterring influence on individual bank expansions. That it can be sufficient would seem to have been borne out in the experiences of such practical examples of competitive note issues as are afforded by the history of the Scotch, Suffolk (Massachusetts) and Canadian systems.[12] Banks in each of these systems seem to have been definitely conscious of the power of holding other banks in check by the return of notes through the clearings.

What influence will the average period for which bank loans in general are made have on the withdrawals in the lag period? It will affect the *rate* of withdrawals. The shorter the average term of all loans outstanding in the banking system the greater will be the withdrawals of cash per week after the expansion, but the shorter will be the lag period, if we assume that the expanding bank has the same average term for its loans as the banking system as a whole. It may be that a sharper pressure on reserves at an early date will

[12] Cf. "U.S. National Monetary Commission, Interviews on the Banking and Currency Systems of Canada," p. 70.

act as a more immediate incentive to the expanding bank to
hold back, and if this is the case it gives some justification for
the principle of *"bankmässige Deckung"* and automatic reflux of notes on which so much emphasis was laid by the
banking and free-banking schools.[13]

Besides questioning the ability of a non-expanding bank to
exercise any control over the expanding banks the central
banking school has also cast doubt on the realism of the concept of the so-called conservative bank and has submitted
that the profit motive may lead all banks to join in an expansion.[14] The term conservative was intended to imply that the
bank for some reason resists the forces causing others to expand credit. If we suppose that there occurs a rise in the
demand for capital (a rise in the "natural" rate of interest) it
is possible for all banks to get out more credit so long as they
keep the market rate of interest at or about its old level, and
if the elasticity of demand for credit is greater than unity the
gross profits of all banks will be greater if they lend more at
the old rates than if they lend the same at a higher rate. If
they lend more, of course, they do it at the expense of a
reduction in their reserve ratios. If all or a majority of them
are unwilling to increase their lending and lower their reserve ratios the market rate of interest will rise towards the
"natural" rate, but the fewer are the number of banks who
insist on retaining their old reserve ratios the smaller will be
the rise in the money rate and the greater the extension in
the volume of credit.

A bank which is conservative must be supposed to foresee
the events following on the boom, so that it anticipates that
the profits it could gain by joining in the boom would be
subsequently counterbalanced by the losses of the crisis

---

[13] See p. 174 of this chapter.
[14] See Neisser, "Notenbankfreiheit?" in the *Weltwirtschaftliches Archiv.*, October, 1930, pp. 449–50. Also Carl Landauer, "Bankfreiheit?" in *Der deutsche
Volkswirt*, September 7th, 1928.

when credit customers withdraw cash and debtor customers are unable to repay their loans. But it has been suggested that such banks, even though they are fully aware of all the consequences of an expansion, will not have any incentive to hold off from it, because they will find that the profits of the boom more than compensate for the losses of the crisis and depression; and the larger is the number of the banks who want to expand, whether because they do not foresee the crisis and depression or because they compute the gains as greater than the losses, the more unprofitable will it be for any individual bank to stay out, since it has small chance of escaping entirely from the effects of the crisis brought about by the policy of its rivals.[15] This argument is however still open to the question whether it is likely that the profits would exceed the losses, and therefore whether there would be many banks willing to lower their reserve ratios, if there were no central bank to give external aid during the crisis *and* the banks were always under the threat of liquidation in the case of a suspension of specie payments. The risk necessary to take in order to make the extra profits in the boom would include the possibility of insolvency.

The third argument, advanced in favour of central banking, is that a central banking institution has by reason of the confidence placed in it by the public the power to mollify the difficulties of a crisis. It was explained that in a crisis the banks in a free-banking system would be under pressure from their creditors for payment in cash and would be compelled, in consideration of the safety of their own reserve position, to contract their lending. All banks would be doing the same and borrowers previously accommodated by them would be forced into liquidation. Many of the banks them-

---

[15] The only chance the minority have of escaping is if they have been able to select their assets so carefully that they are easily realisable even in the crisis, and if their more liquid position is sufficient to retain the confidence of the public, so that instead of their having deposits withdrawn they actually receive new deposits transferred to them from other banks.

selves must fail in the process. No bank would be willing to increase its circulation for fear of getting more notes brought back for gold and there would be no other lending agency to ease the situation. If there is a central bank, on the other hand, such a bank can increase its circulation in the crisis without fearing an internal demand for gold, since people are willing to accept its notes without question. The gaps that would otherwise be left by the commercial banks in the credit structure when the crisis constrains them to draw in their loans, can therefore be filled by the central bank acting as the lender of last resort. It can carry out this function of making the market more liquid either by lending direct to the banks or by lending to those who are called on by the banks for repayment.[16]

When the public withdraws large quantities of cash from the banks the lender of last resort lends to fill the deficiencies. This doctrine is one which establishes the practical rule of banking policy, that in time of a crisis the lender of last resort should lend freely on good security at a high rate of interest. Its action implies technically an increase in the total amount of money, but this is held to be harmless at such times and in no way inflationary, because the additional cash merely goes into hoards and is not used to increase the volume of money coming forward in purchase of goods, and so long as the rate of discount is high the amount borrowed is kept well within these limits, while at the same time deposits are attracted back to the banks. The addition made to

---

[16] Going off the gold standard assists the commercial banks in a direct way, as it no doubt did in this country in 1931. The withdrawal of balances to abroad, in so far as it takes place via an export of gold, sees a reduction in the reserves of the banks at the Bank of England unless the latter is in a position to offset, which it cannot do if the external drain of gold is exceptionally heavy. If it goes off the gold standard there is no need for any offsetting. The exporter of capital cannot withdraw gold from the Bank; he must buy foreign exchange at an enhanced rate, and there is merely a transfer between deposits at the banks from his account to the account of the seller of foreign exchange and the bankers' balances at the Bank of England suffer no net change.

cash resources by the central bank in time of crisis allays the tendency to a panic and slows up what would otherwise develop into a chronic process of liquidation.

If crises are bound to occur under either system this becomes, according to the one school, in itself adequate reason for preferring a central banking organisation to a free-banking one. The free-banking school has sometimes opposed to this the counter-argument[17] that if a central or other institution regularly gives aid whenever the money market is in difficulties, the knowledge that this is continually to be relied upon will become part of the *data* anticipated by the commercial banks and will itself be a reason why they will expand their lending operations beyond the limits which would give them the margin of safety consistent with a dependence entirely on their own resources, and if distress support ceased to be given and banks were allowed to crash if they were unable to keep going by self-help, the disorders giving rise to a crisis would in future not occur. This counter-argument is weakened if we have to assume that, given the fact that there will be some banks who expand credit unwisely until their solvency becomes suspect, the non-expanding banks cannot escape entirely from the evil impact of the policy followed by their less cautious rivals, and if anything in the nature of a panic starts it is likely to affect all to such an extent that even the prudent banks may not be able to keep above water since no bank can be 100 percent liquid. Unless it can be proved that free banking would entirely eliminate the trade cycle and general runs on the banks, the argument for the lender of last resort remains a very powerful argument in defence of central banking.[18]

[17] See Mises, "Geldwertstabilisierung und Konjunkturpolitik," pp. 62–63.

[18] The case might be analysed along Pigovian lines (see "Economics of Welfare," 4th Edition, Part II., Chapter IX., Section 10) as one where uncompensated damage is inflicted by the guilty banks on their innocent rivals, and as such giving grounds for some kind of intervention.

Before proceeding to the fourth and fifth arguments in favour of central banking, we may digress here to consider what was the relation of the arguments we have already discussed to two subsidiary problems: the prohibition of small notes and the justification of the exclusion of deposit banking from the strictures applied to the note issue.

The arguments we have so far examined in connection with the note issue in general were held to apply a *fortiori* to the case of notes of low denomination. Small notes were, in the first place, particularly liable to come into the hands of the poorer and more ignorant classes who were most unable to discriminate between the issuers. In the second place they tend to return less frequently to the banks and so are not often put to the test of convertibility, whereas the larger notes not only come back for change but are also mainly in the hands of those who make and receive large payments and are most likely to use them in transactions with the banks. Again, while in normal times small notes are seldom converted, they become particularly dangerous at the least sign of alarm, because it is the poorer and more uneducated people who are the first to "panic."[19] We notice that even Wagner, who was in favour of keeping restrictions at a minimum, thought that the prohibition of small notes might be wise in a free-banking system.

Most of the supporters of restrictions on freedom to issue notes conceded that the same strictures did not need to be applied to deposit banking, and many of them fought enthusiastically for freedom in this sphere.

Various reasons were offered at different stages in the development of currency and credit doctrine as to why deposit banking came into another category than that of the issue of notes. The distinction was first supported on the grounds that notes were money and deposits subject to

[19] See, for example, Horsley Palmer's evidence before the 1832 Commission, Q. 273, where he objects to £1 notes on these grounds.

check were not, and therefore they did not have the same effect on prices. Other writers based it on the less fallacious reasoning that the public had less choice in accepting notes than in accepting checks. Later, it was attributed to the circumstance that the creation of deposits is more subject than that of bank-notes to the redemption check via interbank clearings. Finally, it has been justified by reference to the proposition that the control over the creation of bank-notes gives the central bank indirect control over the amount of deposits as well, since central bank money constitutes the cash reserves of the deposit banks.

Two subsidiary arguments in favour of central banks have become prominent, especially in post-war years. The first of these claims that we must have some central monetary authority in order that we may pursue what is called a "rational" monetary policy.

The policy of the central bank is no longer conceived to be automatic in the manner envisaged by the founders of the currency school. The volume of circulating media does not change in response to specie movements. These may be ignored or offset as the central bank management thinks fit. With the aid of discount rate and open market operations it adopts an active policy of increasing or decreasing the cash reserves of the money market and the total volume of credit. We retain in this country merely a semblance of the principle underlying the Act of 1844. If the deposits the Bank creates cause, in the course of time, a demand for notes which it cannot supply under the fixed fiduciary issue, it can rely on a suspension of Peel's Act; if they cause an increase in foreign claims and a drain of its gold reserves, it can go off the gold standard.

Out of the realisation of the central bank's power to determine the volume of credit there arose the notion that it should consciously direct monetary policy along "scientific lines." The question then arises: What is to be the criterion of this "scientific" management? The criterion which has so far usually been adopted, namely, that of the stability of the general price level, has been suspect in theory and just as unfortunate in practice. Although the contributions of Mises, Hayek, Keynes, Myrdahl[20] and others have gone far to elucidate the forces at work, we have yet to wait for the formulation of some other criterion in clearly delineated enough terms to allow of its adoption as a rule of monetary policy. Meanwhile, it is the efficacy of central bank control rather than the objective so far followed that is most called into question by monetary reformers, and consequently the demand is raised for the concentration of still more control in the hands of the central monetary authority by extending its direct control to deposits as well as the note issue.

The other argument is of a similar nature. It looks on the central bank as an essential instrument for securing international co-operation in monetary policy. In the past, at least, this has usually meant arriving at understandings in the field of discount policy to obviate the necessity of a deflation in a country which, under the rules of the gold standard, should undergo a decrease in its money incomes. As such it is regarded as an essential link in price stabilisation policy. Thus Mr. Hawtrey[21] conceives of it as a means of surmounting the difficulties raised by the circumstance that stable exchange rates between countries may not always be compatible with a stable price level within each separate country. If the level in one country A is to be kept stable, it may be necessary to have a rise in country B, or, alternatively, if B's price level is to be kept stable, there may have to be a fall

---

[20] L. von Mises, "The Theory of Money" and "Geldwertstabilisierung und Konjunkturpolitik"; F. A. von Hayek, "Monetary Theory and the Trade Cycle" and "Prices and Production"; J. M. Keynes, "Treatise on Money"; G. Myrdahl, "Der Gleichgewichtsbegriff als Instrument der geldtheoretischen Analyse," and T. Koopmans, "Zum Problem des 'neutralen' Geldes," in "Beiträge zur Geldtheorie," edited by F. A. von Hayek.

[21] See "Monetary Reconstruction," pp. 144-5.

in country A. He looks to arrangements between central banks to determine how "these departures from the norm" can best be distributed between the countries concerned.

The securing of international co-operation was hinted at as being the most important modern function of central banks both at the Brussels Conference in 1920[22] and at the Genoa Conference in 1922.[23] Central bank leaders see it in the same strong light, and we find Mr. Montagu Norman describing his efforts to bring about co-operation among the central banks of the world as one of his two main tasks during recent years.[24] That his efforts did not go unrecognised is evidenced by the widespread opinion that the forcing down of discount rates by the Federal Reserve in the latter half of 1927 took place under persuasion from representatives of other central banks.[25] But more impressive results are evidently envisaged by those who deplore the fact that co-operation has not yet succeeded in going much beyond "an *ad hoc* agreement that certain steps may be taken about rates."[26] If it were really true that central bank co-operation is directed towards the observation of the rules of the "gold standard game," as some of its disciples pretend,[27] there would, even if there were nothing to be said in its favour, be at least nothing to be said against it. In effect, however, the theory underlying it amounts to a complete negation of the principles under which the international gold standard works.

Less objectionable would seem to be that aspect of international co-operation which has had a long history of practical application and which is an extension of the concept of

---

[22] International Financial Conference.

[23] International Economic Conference.

[24] "MacMillan Committee, Minutes of Evidence," 3317.

[25] See "Committee on National and Federal Reserve Systems," U.S.A., 1931, pp. 162, 213–14.

[26] "MacMillan Committee, Minutes of Evidence," 6720 (Sir Otto Niemeyer).

[27] *Ibid.,* 1597 (Sir Robert Kindersley).

the "lender of last resort" to the international sphere. Where the banking system of any country is faced by a run of foreign depositors, the assistance which can be rendered by the central bank of that country to the deposit banks may not be able to go very far on the basis of its own gold reserves, and it has not infrequently happened in the past that a foreign central bank or group of foreign banks has lent funds to the central bank in difficulties. Mr. Hawtrey looks forward to the time when this function of the international lender of last resort will be assumed by the Bank for International Settlements.[28]

The two arguments last mentioned have become in our time the almost exclusively motivating reasons for the foundations of new central banks. A clear example of this is to be found in the recommendations of the recent Royal Commission on Banking and Currency in Canada.[29] They are characteristic of the change that has taken place in the theory of central banking. The classical theory of central banking was that it should make monetary movements as far as possible automatic. The modern theory is to substitute "intelligent planning" for automatic rules. To those who would prefer to place their trust in semi-automatic forces rather than in the wits of central bank managers and their advisers, free banking would appear to be by far the lesser evil. Banks which have not the possibility of abrogating their liability to pay their obligations in gold cannot go very far wide of the path following movements in their gold reserves.

Any attempt to make a final evaluation of the relative merits of alternative systems of banking must look primarily to the tendencies they manifest towards instability, or more particularly to the amount of causal influence they exert in cyclical fluctuations. Most modern theories of the trade cycle seek the originating force of booms and depressions in

[28] R. G. Hawtrey, "The Art of Central Banking," p. 228.
[29] 1933. See the Commission's Report, pp. 62–64.

credit expansions and contractions with the banks as the engineering agencies. A more comprehensive view considers that these movements are not features exclusively of the banking system, but that, while liable to be aggravated by the banking system, they will occur under any monetary system.

It was apparently assumed by writers of the currency school[30] that with a purely metallic currency, and therefore with a strict operation of the currency principle, there would be no disequilibrating monetary factors. In this connection there was some valid point in the classical theory of the hoards. The banking school held that even in a purely metallic currency where there is no creation of bank credit, the effective circulation will still vary with the movements of money in and out of what they called the hoards.[31] Modern theory essentially generalises this concept to cover all changes in the rate of spending cash balances in general, and comes to the conclusion that it is possible that these fluctuations in the effective circulation which come about as the result of spontaneous action on the part of the public may be sufficient to generate cyclical fluctuations in business activity without the guilt of the banks.

It is difficult to judge how great would be these primary changes in the public's demand for cash: the movements which have recently made such a marked impression on the financial structure have arisen largely as secondary movements consequent on prior disturbances in the banking system. They were caused either directly or indirectly by credit expansions and contractions. The non-existence of a banking system would eliminate the very large element caused by panic hoarding, but there would remain such fac-

---

[30] Particularly Tellkampf and Geyer.

[31] See, e.g., Fullarton, "On the Regulation of Currencies," pp. 138–41; A. Wagner, "Beiträge zur Lehre von den Banken," p. 126; J. S. Mill, "Principles of Political Economy," Vol. II., Bk. II., pp. 204, 210–11.

tors as integrations and disintegrations in industry, changes in population, alterations in the attitude of the public towards different risk distributions of their assets. If these "natural" accelerations and decelerations in the turnover of balances are likely to reach appreciable dimensions, then it may become part of the object and usefulness of banking to counteract them, and a fiduciary issue (whether in the form of uncovered notes or of check deposits) may, we find, be a necessity, if monetary factors are to be kept neutral.

How to discover a banking system which will not be the cause of catastrophic disturbances, which is least likely itself to introduce oscillations and most likely to make the correct adjustments to counteract changes from the side of the public, is the most acute unsettled economic problem of our day.

There is not much doubt that the present banking system is actively responsible for disturbances. The more difficult task is to determine out of what particular features of the system they arise. But it seems to be an indisputable fact that the major fluctuations come from changes in the amount of cash provided by the central banks. We find that the commercial banks keep relatively stable reserve proportions and that their lending activities follow fairly closely (except in the pit of the depression) movements in central bank money.[32] These movements are, of course, magnified by the coefficient of expansion, say, ten times, but central bank policy is always conducted with the knowledge of this fact in mind. It is propositions of this kind which seem to lend support to the theory, most recently put forward by Mises,[33]

[32] Between November, 1925, and March, 1935, the monthly figures of the average percentage of cash to deposits held by the London Clearing Banks showed an absolute range of between a maximum of 12.0 percent and a minimum of 10.0 percent. During the same period the Bank of England "proportion" showed a range of 65.5 to 11.5 percent, and, even ignoring these extremes, fluctuations between 50 and 30 percent, or even 25 percent, may be considered as quite a normal spread.

[33] "Geldwertstabilisierung und Konjunkturpolitik," p. 61.

that fluctuations, while not being entirely eliminated, would be much reduced under free banking. And it is undoubtedly true that such a system is much less capable of monetary manipulation than a system of central control.

But whatever may be our verdict as to the comparative outcome of the two systems in terms of stability it is unlikely that the choice can ever again become a practical one. To the vast majority of people government interference in matters of banking has become so much an integral part of the accepted institutions that to suggest its abandonment is to invite ridicule. One result of this attitude is that insolvency in the sphere of banking has won exception from the rule applied in other lines of business that it must be paid for by liquidation, and it is important also to point out that since the laws of bankruptcy have almost never been strictly applied to banking we should be diffident of drawing the conclusion that actual experiences prove the unworkability of free competition in banking.

Such pleas as are occasionally made in our day for free trade in banking come from sources which do not commend them. They are the product of theories of "money magic." Their demand for free banking is based on the notion that it would provide practically unlimited supplies of credit and they ascribe all industrial and social evils to deficiencies of banking caused by bank monopoly.[34] As a matter of practical policy the tendencies are all in the direction of increased centralisation. When the choice was made in the nineteenth century in favour of controlling the note issue, deposit banking was for various reasons left "free." At the present time there are signs of an approaching extension of the control to deposits. This would secure the final concentration of monetary power in the hands of the central authority and would be the consistent outcome of central bank philosophy and

[34] See Hake and Wesslau, "Free Trade in Capital," 1890; Henry Meulen, "Free Banking" (1st Edition, 1917, 2nd Edition, revised, 1934).

the currency doctrine. There are already strong movements in this direction in both Germany and the United States. In the United States it is as yet only a plan,[35] in Germany it is an accomplished fact.

[35] See the Chicago 100 percent Plan for Banking Reform, an account of which is given by A. G. Hart in an article entitled "The Chicago Plan" of Banking Reform in the *Review of Economic Studies*, February, 1935.

Appendix

On the Working of the "Automatic Mechanism" of Credit Control

In order to make clear the argument on pp. 178–184 of the last chapter we append the following arithmetical example:

1. THE NOTE-ISSUING CASE

Assume that there are two banks (or groups of banks), A and B. Both carry on the same volume of business in the first instance. Each lends 10,000 and has 10,000 loans falling due on each settlement day.

A now increases its lending on a given day by 10,000 and all these extra loans fall due for repayment four clearing periods later, so that there are three clearings in between. Assume further (a) that if B draws gold from A, B does not immediately increase its note issue to the extent that would bring its reserve ratio back to its former level, but only to the extent necessary to replace the notes that have not come in as usual, but have stayed out in the circulation (this merely makes it possible for it to lend currently the same amount as before); (b) that A correspondingly reduces its outstanding note issue by the amount of the loss of gold, that is, by the amount of extra notes it has returned to it by B through the clearings. Then the total note issue outstanding of A and B together remains the same throughout the period under consideration.

Original Position

	A.	B.
Notes	40,000	40,000
Gold	4,000	4,000
Loan repayments	10,000	10,000

A receives 5,000 of its own notes and 5,000 of B's.
B   „   „   „   „   „   A's.
Notes are therefore cleared without any transfer of gold.

Position at First Clearing after A's Expansion

	A.	B.
Notes	50,000	40,000
Gold	4,000	4,000
Loan repayments	10,000	10,000

A receives 5,555 of its own notes and 4,444 of B's.
B   „   4,444   „   „   „   5,555 „ A's.
B draws 1,111 gold from A.

Second Clearing

	A.	B.
Notes	48,889	41,111
Gold	2,889	5,111
Loan repayments	10,000	10,000

A receives 5,433 of its own notes and 4,567 of B's.
B   „   4,567   „   „   „   5,433 „ A's.
B draws 826 gold from A.

Third Clearing

	A.	B.
Notes	48,063	41,937
Gold	2,063	5,937
Loan repayments	10,000	10,000

A receives 5,341 of its own notes and 4,659 of B's.
B ,, 4,659 ,, ,, ,, 5,341 ,, A's.
B draws 682 gold from A.

Fourth Clearing

	A.	B.
Notes	47,381	42,619
Gold	1,381	6,619
Loan repayments	20,000	10,000

A receives 10,530 of its own notes and 9,470 of B's.
B ,, 4,735 ,, ,, ,, 5,265 ,, A's.
B *loses* 4,205 gold to A.

At the end of the fourth clearing the position is:

	A.	B.
Notes	51,586	38,414
Gold	5,586	2,414

2. THE DEPOSIT CREDIT CASE

We may assume in this case that the recipients of checks paid out by the borrowers of the additional 10,000 pay these checks into their banks for collection immediately. It is reasonable to suppose, unless there is an uneven distribution of deposit business between the two banks, that half of these checks will be paid into each bank.

Original Position

	A.	B.
Deposits	40,000	40,000
Cash	4,000	4,000

Position at First Clearing

	A.	B.
Deposits	50,000	40,000
Cash	4,000	4,000

B receives 5,000 in checks drawn on A against which there is no counterclaim of A on B; B therefore claims 5,000 in cash from A.

The position after the first clearing is already untenable for A:

	A.	B.
Deposits	45,000	45,000
Cash	−1,000	8,000 + 1,000

Bibliography

Andréadès, A. *History of the Bank of England.* Translated by Christabel Meredith. London: P. S. King, 1909.

Aretz, Peter. *Die Entwicklung der Diskontpolitik der Bank von England, 1780–1850; eine kritische Studie aus dem Notenbank- und Papiergeldwesen.* Berlin: C. Heymann, 1916.

Aubry, Maurice. *Les Banques d'Emission et d'Escompte.* Paris: Guillaumin, 1864.

Bagehot, Walter. *Lombard Street.* London: Henry S. King, 1873.

Beckhart, Benjamin Haggott. *The Discount Policy of the Federal Reserve System.* New York: Henry Holt, 1924.

Burgess, W. Randolph. *The Reserve Banks and the Money Market.* New York: Harper & Brothers, 1927.

Cairnes, John E. *An Examination into the Principles of Currency Involved in the Bank Charter Act of 1844.* Dublin: Hodges and Smith, 1854.

Canada. Royal Commission on Banking and Currency in Canada. *Report of the Royal Commission on Banking and Currency in Canada.* Ottawa: J. O. Patenaude, 1933.

Carey, Henry C. *The Credit System in France, Great Britain, and the United States.* Philadelphia: Carey, Lea, & Blanchard, 1838.

Cernuschi, Henri. *Contre le Billet de Banque.* Paris: Guillaumin, 1866.

Cernuschi, Henri. *Mécanique de l'Echange.* Paris: A. Lacroix, 1865.

Chevalier, Michel. *Lettres sur l'Amerique du Nord.* Paris: Gosselin, 1837.

Cieszkowski, Auguste. *Du Crédit et de la Circulation.* Paris: Treuttel et Wurtz, 1839.

Coq, Paul. *La Circulation en Banque ou l'Impasse du Monopole.* Paris: Guillaumin, 1865.

Coquelin, Charles. *Le Crédit et les Banques,* 3rd ed. Paris: Guillaumin, 1876 (Preface and annotation by Jean-Gustave Courcelle-Seneuil.)

Coullet, Paul Jacques. *Etudes sur la Circulation Monétaire, la Banque et le Crédit.* Paris: Furne, 1865.

Courcelle-Seneuil, Jean-Gustave. *La Banque Libre.* Paris: Guillaumin, 1867.

Courcelle-Seneuil, Jean-Gustave. *Traité Théorique et Pratique des Opérations de Banque.* Paris: Guillaumin, 1853.

Courtois fils, Alphonse. *Histoire des Banques en France.* Paris: Guillaumin, 1875.

Däbritz, Walther. *Gründung und Anfänge der Disconto-Gesellschaft Berlin. Ein Beitrag zur Bank- und Wirtschaftsgeschichte Deutschlands in den Jahren 1850 bis 1875.* Munich and Leipzig: Duncker & Humblot, 1931.

Die Entwicklung der deutschen Volkswirtschaftslehre im neunzehnten Jahrhundert. Gustav Schmoller zur siebenzigsten Wiederkehr seines Geburtstages, 24. Juni 1908, in Verehrung dargebracht von S. P. Altmann, W. J. Ashley, C. Ballod, *et al.* Leipzig: Duncker & Humblot, 1908.

The Dublin University Magazine, 1840.

Dunbar, Charles Franklin. *Economic Essays.* Edited by O. M. W. Sprague. London: Macmillan, 1904.

Dunbar, Charles Franklin. *The Theory and History of Banking,* 5th ed. Revised by Oliver M. W. Sprague. New York: G. P. Putnam's Sons, 1929.

Du Puynode, Gustave. *De la monnaie du crédit et de l'Impôt.* Paris: Guillaumin, 1853.

Duran, Etienne. *Encore la Question des Banques.* Paris: Guillaumin, 1865.

The Economist.

Enquête sur les principes et les faits généraux qui régissent la circulation monétaire et fiduciaire, 1865–66. 6 vol. Paris: Imprimerie Impériale, 1867.

Fanno, Mar. *Le banche e il mercato monetario.* Rome: Athenaeum, 1912.

Feavearyear, A. E. *The Pound Sterling: A History of English Money.* London: Oxford University Press, 1931.

Fraser's Magazine, 1868.

Fullarton, John. *On the Regulation of Currencies,* 2nd ed. London: John Murray, 1845.

Gallatin, Albert. *Considerations on the Currency and Banking System of the United States.* Philadelphia: Carey & Lea, 1831.

Gallatin, Albert. *Suggestions on the Banks and Currency of the Several United States.* New York: Wiley and Putnam, 1841.

Gerstner, Franz Anton Ritter von. *Berichte aus den Vereinigten Staaten von Nordamerika, über Eisenbahnen, Dampfschiffahrten, Banken und andere öffentliche Unternehmungen.* Leipzig, 1839.

Geyer, Philipp. *Banken und Krisen.* Leipzig: T. O. Weigel, 1865.

Geyer, Philipp. *Theorie und Praxis des Zettelbankwesens nebst einer Charakteristik der engl., französ. und preuss. Bank.* Munich: Fleischmann's Buchhandlung, 1867.

Goschen, [George J.], Viscount. *Essays and Addresses on Economic Questions* (1865–93). London: E. Arnold, 1905.

Goschen, [George J.], Viscount. *The Theory of the Foreign Exchanges.* London: E. Wilson, 1861.

Great Britain. Committee on Finance and Industry. *Minutes of Evidence.* London: H. M. Stationery Office, 1931.

Great Britain. Committee on Finance and Industry. *Report.* London: H. M. Stationery Office, 1931.

Great Britain. House of Commons. Select Committee on Bank Acts. *Report from the Select Committee on Bank Acts.* London: [House of Commons] 1857.

Gregory, T. E., ed. *Select Statutes, Documents and Reports Relating to British Banking, 1832–1928.* Oxford: Oxford University Press, 1929.

Guthrie, George. *Bank Monopoly the Cause of Commercial Crises.* Edinburgh: W. Blackwood and Sons, 1864.

Hake, A. Egmont, and O. E. Wesslau. *Free Trade in Capital.* London: Remington, 1890.

Handwörterbuch des Bankwesens. Herausgegeben von Melchior Palyi and Paul Quittner. Berlin: J. Springer, 1933.

Hankey, Thomson. *Principles of Banking,* 2nd ed. London: E. Wilson, 1873.

Hawtrey, R. G. *The Art of Central Banking.* London: Longmans, Green, 1932.

Hawtrey, R. G. *Monetary Reconstruction,* 2nd ed. London: Longmans, Green, 1926.

Helander, Sven. *Theorie und Politik der Zentralnotenbanken in ihrer Entwicklung.* Jena: G. Fischer, 1916.

[Higgs, Henry, ed.] *Political Economy Club,* vol. 6. London: Macmillan, 1921.

Hildreth, Richard. *The History of Banks: To Which Is Added a Demonstration of the Advantages and Necessity of Free Competition in the Business of Banking.* Boston: Hilliard, Gray, 1837.

Horn, J. Edouard. *La Liberté des Banques*. Paris: Guillaumin, 1866.

Hübner, Otto. *Die Banken*. Leipzig: Hübner, 1853, 1854.

Joplin, Thomas. *An Essay on the General Principles and Present Practice of Banking, in England and Scotland*. Newcastle-upon-Tyne: Edward Walker, 1822.

Le Journal des Economistes.

Juglar, Clément. *Du Change et de la Liberté d'Emission*. Paris: Guillaumin, 1868.

Juglar, Clément. *Des Crises Commerciales et de leur Retour Périodique en France, en Angleterre et aux Etats Unis*. Paris: Guillaumin, 1862.

Kemmerer, Edwin Walter. *The A B C of the Federal Reserve System*, 9th ed. Princeton: Princeton University Press, 1932.

Knies, Carl. *Geld und Kredit*. Berlin: Weidmann'sche Buchhandlung, 1873, 1876, 1879.

Landauer, Carl. "Bankfreiheit?" *Der deutsche Volkswirt. Zeitschrift für Politik und Wirtschaft*, no. 49 (Sept. 7, 1928): 1670–73.

Lasker, Leopold. *Bankfreiheit oder nicht? Mit besonderer Rücksicht auf Preussen und Deutschland*. Berlin: J. Springer Verlag, 1871.

Laughlin, J. Laurence, ed. *Banking Reform*. Chicago: National Citizens' League, 1912.

Laveleye, Emile de. *Le Marché Monétaire et ses Crises depuis Cinquante Ans*. Paris: Guillaumin, 1865.

Liesse, André. *Evolution of Credit and Banks in France from the Founding of the Bank of France to the Present Time*. Washington: Government Printing Office, 1910.

Lotz, Walther. *Geschichte und Kritik des deutschen Bankgesetzes vom 14. März 1875*. Leipzig: Duncker & Humblot, 1888.

Loyd, Samuel Jones [Lord Overstone]. *Tracts and Other Publications on Metallic and Paper Currency*. Edited by J. R. McCulloch. London: n. p., 1857. (Contains material originally published 1837–57.)

Macleod, Henry Dunning. *The Theory and Practice of Banking*. London: Longman, Brown, Green, and Longmans, 1855.

Marqfoy, Gustave. *La Banque de France dans ses Rapports avec le Crédit et la Circulation*. Paris: Guillaumin, 1862.

[McCulloch, J. R.] *Historical Sketch of the Bank of England*. London: Longman, Rees, Orme, Brown, and Green, 1831.

McCulloch, J. R. *A Treatise on Metallic and Paper Money and Banks*. Edinburgh: A. & C. Black, 1858.

Meulen, Henry. *Free Banking*. London: Macmillan, 1934.

Michaelis, Otto. *Volkswirthschaftliche Schriften. vol. 1: Eisenbahn-*

fragen. Handelskrisis von 1857. vol. 2: Von der Börse. Über Staats-anleihen. Theoretisches. Bankfragen. Berlin: Herbig, 1873.

Mill, John Stuart. *Principles of Political Economy.* London: J. W. Parker, 1848.

Miller, Harry E. *Banking Theories in the United States Before 1860.* Cambridge, Mass.: Harvard University Press, 1927.

Mills, Richard Horner. *The Principles of Currency and Banking,* 2nd ed. London: Groombridge and Sons, 1857.

Mises, Ludwig von. *Geldwertstabilisierung und Konjunkturpolitik.* Jena: G. Fischer, 1928.

Mitchell, Wesley Clair. *A History of the Greenbacks, with Special Reference to the Economic Consequences of Their Issue: 1862–65.* Chicago: University of Chicago Press, 1903.

Nasse, Erwin. *Die preussische Bank und die Ausdehnung ihres Geschäftskreises in Deutschland.* Bonn: A. Marcus, 1866.

National Monetary Commission, Publications, 1910–12

Aldrich, Nelson W. *An Address by Senator Nelson W. Aldrich Before the Economic Club of New York, November 29, 1909, on the Work of the National Monetary Commission.* Washington: Government Printing Office, 1910.

Davis, Andrew McFarland. *The Origins of the National Banking System.* Washington: Government Printing Office, 1910.

Dewey, Davis R. *State Banking Before the Civil War.* Washington: Government Printing Office, 1910.

Kinley, David. *The Independent Treasury of the United States and Its Relations to the Banks of the Country.* Washington: Government Printing Office, 1910.

Sprague, O. M. W., *History of Crises Under the National Banking System.* Washington: Government Printing Office, 1910.

Warburg, Paul M. *The Discount System in Europe.* Washington: Government Printing Office, 1910.

U.S. National Monetary Commission. *Interviews on the Banking and Currency Systems of Canada.* Washington: Government Printing Office, 1910.

U.S. National Monetary Commission. *Interviews on the Banking and Currency Systems of England, Scotland, France, Germany, Switzerland, and Italy.* Washington: Government Printing Office, 1910.

Neisser, Hans. "Notenbankfreiheit?" *Weltwirtschaftliches Archiv* 32 (1930 II): 446–61.

Norman, George Warde. *Remarks upon Some Prevalent Errors with Respect to Currency and Banking*. London: Pelham Richardson, 1838.

Palmer, J. Horsley. *The Causes and Consequences of the Pressure upon the Money-Market*. London: Pelham Richardson, 1837.

Parnell, Henry. *Observations on Paper Money, Banking and Overtrading*. London: James Ridgway, 1827.

Parnell, Henry. *A Plain Statement of the Power of the Bank of England and the Use It Has Made of It*. London: James Ridgway, 1832.

Patterson, R. H. *The Economy of Capital*. Edinburgh: W. Blackwood and Sons, 1865.

Pereire, Isaac. *La Banque de France et l'Organisation du Crédit en France*. Paris: P. Dupont, 1864.

Phillips, Chester Arthur. *Bank Credit*. New York: Macmillan, 1920.

Phillips, Edmund. *A Plea for the Reform of the British Currency and Bank of England Charter*. London: Whittaker, 1861.

Poschinger, Heinrich von. *Bankwesen und Bankpolitik in Preussen* 3 vols. Berlin: J. Springer, 1878–79.

Price, Bonamy. *The Principles of Currency*. Oxford: J. Parker, 1869.

Raguet, Condy. *A Treatise on Currency and Banking*. Philadelphia: Grigg & Elliot, 1839.

Ramon, Gabriel. *Histoire de la Banque de France*. Paris: Bernard Grasset, 1929.

Report from the Committee of Secrecy on the Bank of England Charter, 1831–32.

Reports by the Lords Committees Appointed a Secret Committee to enquire into the State of the Bank of England, with respect to the Expediency of the Resumption of Cash Payments. Parliamentary Papers 1819 (291), vol. III.

La Revue des Deux-Mondes.

Richards, R. D. *The Early History of Banking in England*. London: P. S. King, 1929.

Scharling, William. *Bankpolitik*. Jena: G. Fischer, 1900.

Spencer, Herbert. *Essays, Scientific, Political, and Speculative*. New York: D. Appleton, 1891.

Sprague, O. M. W. *Banking Reform in the United States*. Cambridge, Mass.: Harvard University Press, 1911.

Sumner, William Graham, et al. *A History of Banking in All the Leading Nations*. 4 vols. New York: The Journal of Commerce and Commercial Bulletin, 1896.

Tellkampf, J. L. *Essays on Law Reform, Commercial Policy, Banks, Peni-

tentiaries, etc., in Great Britain and the United States of America. London: Williams & Norgate, 1859.

Tellkampf, Johann Ludwig. *Die Prinzipien des Geld- und Bankwesens.* Berlin: Puttkammer & Mühlbrecht, 1867.

Tellkampf, Johann Ludwig. *Über die neuere Entwicklung des Bankwesens in Deutschland mit Hinweis auf dessen Vorbilder in England, Schottland, und Nordamerika und auf die französische Société générale de Crédit mobilier.* 4th ed. Breslau: Morgenstern, 1857.

Tippetts, Charles S. *State Banks and the Federal Reserve System.* New York: D. Van Nostrand, 1929.

Tooke, Thomas. *A History of Prices* [vol. 3]. London: Longman et al., 1840.

U.S. Comptroller of the Currency. *Annual Reports.* Washington: Government Printing Office.

U.S. Congress. Senate. Committee on Banking and Currency. *Banking and Currency. Hearings . . . on . . . a Bill to Provide for the Establishment of Federal Reserve Banks.* 3 vols. Washington: Government Printing Office, 1913.

U.S. Congress. Senate. Committee on Banking and Currency. *Operation of the National and Federal Reserve Banking Systems. Hearings . . .* Washington: Government Printing Office, 1931.

Vierteljahresschrift für Volkswirthschaft und Kulturgeschichte. Herausgegeben von Julius Faucher, Otto Michaelis, et al., 1863 and 1865.

Wagner, Adolph. *Beiträge zur Lehre von den Banken.* Leipzig: Voss, 1857.

Wagner, Adolph. *Die Geld- und Credittheorie der Peel'schen Bankacte.* Vienna: Braumüller, 1862.

Wagner, Adolph. *System der deutschen Zettelbankgesetzgebung, unter Vergleichung mit der ausländischen. Zugleich ein Handbuch des Zettlebankwesens. Mit Rücksicht auf die Errichtung von Zettelbanken in Baden, sowie die Bankreform und das Staatspapiergeldwesen im norddeutschen Bunde.* Freiburg i. Br.: Wagner'sche Buchhandlung, 1870.

Wagner, Adolph. *System der Zettelbankpolitik, mit besonderer Rücksicht auf das geltende Recht und auf deutsche Verhältnisse.* 2. theilweise umgearbeitete und vervollständigte Ausgabe. Freiburg i. Br.: Wagner'sche Buchhandlung, 1873.

White, Horace. *Money and Banking Illustrated by American History,* 5th ed. Boston: Ginn, 1914.

Willis, Henry Parker. *The Federal Reserve System: Legislation, Organization and Operation.* New York: Ronald Press, 1923.

Willis, H. Parker, and John M. Chapman. *The Banking Situation: American Post-war Problems and Developments.* New York: Columbia University Press, 1934.

Wilson, James. *Capital, Currency and Banking.* London: The Economist, 1847.

Wolowski, Louis. *Les Banques d'Angleterre et les Banques d'Ecosse.* Paris: Guillaumin, 1867.

Wolowski, Louis. *La Question des Banques.* Paris: Guillaumin, 1864.

Index

99–100, 105–106, 121–123,
125–126, 128, 133, 136–142,
167
See also Bank-notes;
Competition; Country banks;
Fiduciary issue; Greenback
era; Joint stock banks; Note
redemption; Reserves
Note redemption, 49–50, 54, 56, 73,
75, 178–179

Over-issue of notes. See Note issue

Palmer, J. Horsley, 18n, 19–20, 22,
61n, 72n, 188n
Panic. See Bank runs
Paper currency. See Money
Paper money. See Bank-notes;
Money
Parnell, Henry, 72–74, 76, 77, 79,
144
Patterson, R. H., 102, 134, 135
Peace of Tilsit, 58
Peel, Robert, 22
Peel's Act, 22, 27, 67, 68, 80, 113,
117, 118, 124–126, 189
Peel system. See Fiduciary issue
Pereire brothers, 38–39, 40, 97, 98,
100, 101, 103, 118, 134–135,
138
Philipps, Edmund, 136
Phillips, Chester A., 181n
Pigou, A. C., 187n
Pitt, William, 14–15
Plural banking system, 10, 96–97, 111
notes of, 108–109
See also Competition; Free
banking; Note issue
Political crisis of 1848 (France), 32–35
Political Economy Club, 72, 134
Price, Bonamy, 90–91, 133–134, 144
Private banks
in England, 14, 16–17, 20

in France, 31–33
in Prussia/Germany, 58–59, 60–
62, 65–66, 69–70
in Scotland, 26
Privileged banks. See Central bank;
Government role; Monopoly
Protectionism, 9, 81, 167
Provincial banks. See Country banks
Prussian Bank, 61–69, 124, 130
See also Reichsbank

Quantity theory of money. See
Money

Raguet, Condy, 83–84, 92–93
Real bills doctrine. See Bankmässige
cover; Reflux of notes
principle
Rediscount policy, 166
Reflux of notes principle, 118, 172,
174
See also Bankmässige cover
Reichsbank, 69–70, 128
Reserve centers or cities, 157, 170–
171
Reserve equalisation, 140, 161
Reserves
cash, 19
centralisation of, 106
of currency, 9
drain on, 74–76, 86–87, 124, 135,
161
fixed proportion of, 113, 118,
171
legal ratios, 154–156
metal, 19, 34, 61, 97
pooling of, 140, 161
in specie, 37, 53
Reserve systems, 19, 21, 106, 139–142
Restrictionist school (France), 93
Rossi, Pellegrino L. E., 93
Rouland, M., 36n
Royal Bank of Berlin, 58–61

This book was set in ITC Zapf Book, a typeface designed for the International Typeface Corporation by one of the world's foremost typeface designers, Hermann Zapf. The creator of Optima, Palatino, Melior, Aldus, and many other acclaimed typefaces, Hermann Zapf spent more than two years developing ITC Zapf Book as a family of four different weights of type with matching italics. The elegant letterforms are an artful blend of Walbaum, Melior, and Bodoni, distinguished by many subtle refinements. Hermann Zapf was born in 1918 in Nuremberg, Germany. Designer of more than forty typefaces, his first typeface design was marketed in 1940; ten years later, the first of the famous Palatino type family was introduced. All of his typefaces are characterized by exquisite design, quiet distinction, and innovation without eccentricity. Zapf's primary concern is never with single letters, but with their fusion with each other in a working text. To Zapf, "Type is the tie or ligature between author and reader."

This book is printed on paper that is acid-free and meets the requirements of the American National Standard for Permanence of Paper for Printed Library Materials, Z39.48–1992. ∞

Book design by Hermann Strohbach, New York, New York
Editorial services by Harkavy Publishing Service,
New York, New York
Index by Primary Sources Research, Chevy Chase, Maryland
Typography by Shepard Poorman Communications Corporation,
Indianapolis, Indiana
Printed and bound by Thomson-Shore, Dexter, Michigan